"[Mailer] has created something like a religion. [In *On God*] he lays out his personal vision of what the universe's higher truths might look like. . . . But his theology is not theoretical to him. After eight decades, it is what he believes. He expects no adherents, and does not profess to be a prophet, but he has worked to forge his beliefs into a coherent catechism. . . . In another sense, *On God* is Mailer's own *non serviam*, his disavowal of organized religion. . . . Courage amid uncertainty is, as always, Mailer's highest virtue."   —*New York*

"Thought-provoking . . . deliberate and expressive. [Mailer] stares down God in a series of conversations with his friend and literary executor Lennon. Over ten chapters, the literary giant candidly holds forth on various aspects of faith. . . . Mailer is a pensive and articulate writer, and this conceptual exercise capitalizes and expands on the ideas set forth in his novel *The Castle in the Forest*."   —*Rocky Mountain News*

"Remarkable. [Mailer's] a believer—in his own fashion. . . . Ever since he gave up atheism at thirty, Mailer has been alive to the possibility of the spiritual. Here, he puts on the record his typically idiosyncratic beliefs. . . . He has made [God] into a complex character."   —*The Globe and Mail* (Canada)

On God

ALSO BY NORMAN MAILER

On God

AN UNCOMMON CONVERSATION

Norman Mailer

with Michael Lennon

RANDOM HOUSE TRADE PAPERBACKS

NEW YORK

To my wife, my sister, my children,
and to my grandchildren

Norman Mailer

To my sisters, Kathleen Arruda
and Maureen Macedo

Michael Lennon

CONTENTS

PREFACE

Michael Lennon

The impetus to ask Norman Mailer if he would engage in discussion of his religious beliefs was a reading of an early draft of his novel *The Castle in the Forest*, sometime in the summer or early fall of 2002. Although his novels and narrative nonfiction back to the 1950s are shot through with his ideas on God and the Devil and the struggle in which they are locked, in those works, this material was there largely as a backdrop, a sort of cosmic context for the journeys and struggles of his characters. Before *The Castle in the Forest*, the direct interventions of angels and demons were surmises. But in that work, Dieter, an assistant to the Devil, changed everything. Now Mailer had invested his characters with his beliefs about the tripartite division of power in our solar system among God, the Devil, and humanity. Dieter, as we now

know, narrates the novel and also communicates with the
Devil, whom he refers to as the E.O. (Evil One). On a purely
functional level, his choice of Dieter, who has powers verging
on omniscience, allowed Mailer to retain a first-person voice
and still have access to the thoughts of the Hitler family. After
a half century of tantalizing his readers with glimpses of his
quasi-Gnostic belief in the existential struggle between good
and evil, Mailer decided to present a key battle in this war,
one that took place in Austria at the end of the nineteenth
century.

In the early 1980s, I wrote an essay on Mailer's cosmology,
and I remained persistent in my conviction of the importance
of his idiosyncratic beliefs to serious readers of his work. So I
was excited to read of the demonic and divine machinations
surrounding Hitler's birth and early life. Shortly after I read
the first hundred pages of the novel in draft form, Mailer
asked me to help on a fund-raiser for the Provincetown Theater. He wanted me to play a role in a staged reading of G. B.
Shaw's *Don Juan in Hell*. Mailer was to direct the play and
take the part of Don Juan. His wife, Norris Church Mailer,
was to play Dona Ana, and I was to play her father, the
Commodore. Gore Vidal, in a brilliant bit of casting, was to
take the part of the Devil. Shaw's play is set in Hell, and the
exchanges among the four characters, especially Don Juan
and the Devil, gave me another slant on Mailer's ideas. For
the week of rehearsal preceding the one-night production,
my brain was on fire with speculations about the interplay between the ideas of Mailer and Shaw, not to mention

the fascinating interplay between two novelists who had feuded so famously in the 1970s yet were now collaborating.

In the spring of 2003, I visited Mailer's home in Provincetown and proposed that we begin the conversations collected here. He agreed immediately. His only proviso was that my questions remain with me until we met so that his answers would be spontaneous. (He once said that his favorite word was "improvisational.") The first conversation took place on June 17, 2003, and they continued, sometimes six months apart, until June 14, 2006. All of them took place in the third-floor study of his house, where from the big window one can see the swerve of shore and bend of bay of Provincetown harbor.

The transcripts have been cleaned up a bit, mainly to eliminate redundancies and correct a few names and dates. They are presented in the order in which they took place. The titles given to them are not summative but merely a reflection of my opening questions.

INTRODUCTION

Norman Mailer

In any amateur approach to weighty subjects, the perils are obvious. They need hardly be cited. Yet there is one advantage: You are not obliged to be loyal to the expertise you have studiously acquired, and you do not have to confront the displeasure of one's learned colleagues by forcing them to come face-to-face with a radically new concept.

Of course, amateurs rarely succeed. I offer the interviews that follow as an example. I am obviously ignorant of most of the intellections required of a competent theologian. My colleague in these interviews, Michael Lennon, while not a formal student of the subjects, is at least reasonably well versed in the concepts we discuss. But what will be evident to anyone who has studied such matters is how truly untutored I am.

I offer nothing but my own ideas—which is the classic error of the amateur.

How, then, can I defend this venture? The answer may be legitimate: I have spent the last fifty years trying to contemplate the nature of God. If I speak specifically of fifty years, it is because my pride in the initial thirty-odd years of my life was to be an atheist—how much more difficult and honorable I then considered that to be, rather than having a belief in an All-Mighty divinity. I was a novelist, after all (as will be noted frequently in these interviews), so I was intensely, even professionally, aware of the variety, and complexity, of human motivation and its offspring—morality. It took a good number of years to recognize that I did believe in God—that is, believed there is a divine presence in existence. On occasion, I even contemplated the philosophical need to approach what might be the characteristics of such an enigma. Whenever I tried, however, to advance my notions by readings in theology, I was repelled. The works were studies, for the most part, of the unstated but dictatorial injunction to have faith. They were undernourished in their appetite for inquiry, and full of ideological dicta.

To say again, I am a novelist. The best of us spend our lives exploring what might be human reality. In consequence, the conviction grew that I had a right to believe in the God I could visualize: an imperfect, existential God doing the best He (or She) could manage against all the odds of an existence that not even He, our Creator, entirely controlled. Note the possessive: *our* Creator. God, as I could visualize such a being, was an Artist, not a lawgiver, a mighty source of creative energy, an embattled moralist, a celestial general engaged in a celestial war, but never a divinity who was All-Good and All-Powerful. While I was aware that somewhere on the scholarly horizon a group called "process theologians" were also questioning the perfection of God, my instinct was to continue to work alone in these speculations until Michael Lennon proposed these interviews. Of their shortcomings I am aware and, doubtless, also unaware, but my philosophical reconnaissances are, after all, not so unique. A good part of humanity may also be devoted (usually in deepest privacy) to exploring their intuition of what God and the Devil might be all about. Such people explore all those aspects that no church seems ready to approach.

All apologies now delivered, I invite the reader to these dialogues. I hope (and expect) they will be rewarded with a few new ideas.

On God

I

On God as the Artist

MICHAEL LENNON: *Scientists believe that the universe is expanding. Is this accelerating nature of the cosmos reflected in your concept of a god who can grow and develop?*

NORMAN MAILER: I start from another direction. Having been a novelist all my working life, I may know a little about human beings. I should. They have been my study. You might say my theological notions come out of such questions as, Who are we? What are we? How do we develop? Why, indeed, are we in existence? And is there the presence of a Creator in what we do?

So the larger cosmic speculations are of less interest to me. In truth, I would hate to rely on the ever-changing state of advanced physics for my ideas.

In places, you've said that God and the Devil are lesser divinities in liege to larger powers who might be the ultimate creators. Who or what do you feel is the ultimate power in the universe? Who created the universe?

I feel the same way about the ultimate Creator as I feel about the expanding universe: All that is too large for my speculations. But I don't see any inherent logical contradiction in saying that I do believe our God created the world we live in and is in constant conflict with the Devil.

In St. George and the Godfather, *you say, "The world's more coherent if God exists, and twice coherent if He exists like us." I'm afraid this logic smacks of wish fulfillment. God need not exist merely to satisfy your desire for order. Perhaps the world is incoherent; perhaps the cosmos is disordered.*

Where does my desire for order come from? Not only do we humans have a fundamental desire for order, we have an obvious tendency as well toward disorder—a true conflict between order and disorder. So I say it may be worth the attempt to search into such questions.

That may require hearing your thoughts on the relationship between the nature of the deity and codes for human living.

Oh, Christ, Mike, I don't think in these formulae. I want to get to something more basic to my thought, which is that much of the world's present-day cosmology is based on such works of revelation as the Old and New Testament, or the Koran, yet for me Revelation is itself the question mark. Revelation, after all, is not God's words but ours, words debated back then, if you will, in committee and assembled by working theologians with varying agendas. After all, why would God bother to speak in such a fashion? There's no need. God could have imparted such thoughts directly to us. Revelation has always struck me as a power trip for high priests who were looking to create a product that would enable them to lead their flock more securely, more emphatically. Their modern-day practitioners quote constantly from Scripture on TV, use it as their guide rail, and run into intolerable contradictions that are guaranteed to cripple their power to reason. I will go so far as to say that to be a Fundamentalist is to exist as a human whose reasoning powers have been degraded into inanition before any question for which a Fundamentalist does not already have an answer.

I confess, then, that I feel no attachment whatsoever to organized religion. I see God, rather, as a Creator, as the greatest artist. I see human beings as His most developed artworks. I also see animals as His artworks. When I think of evolution, what stands out most is the drama that went on in God as an artist. Successes were also marred by failures. I think of all the errors He made in evolution as well as of the successes. In marine life, for example, some fish have hideous eyes—they protrude from the head in tubes many inches long. Think of all those animals of the past with their peculiar ugliness, their misshapen bodies, worm life, frog life, vermin life, that myriad of insects—so many unsuccessful experiments. These were also modes the Artist was trying—this great artist, this divine artist—to express something incredible, and it was not, for certain, an easy process. Indeed, it went on forever! I would guess that evolution was tampered with, if not actually blindsided on occasion, by the Devil. I think there were false trips that God engaged in because the Devil deluded Him— or Her. Forgive me if I keep speaking of God as "Him," that's a habit that's come down to me from Revelation. Obviously, to speak of God as "Her" is off-putting, but to speak of "Him/Her" or "It" is worse.

In any event, it makes sense to me that this strife between God and the Devil has been a factor in evolution. Whether God had a free hand or the Devil was meddling in it from the commencement—either way, some species were badly conceived. Sometimes a young artist has to make large errors before he or she can go farther.

I can hear the obvious rejoinder: "There's Norman Mailer, an artist of dubious high rank looking to give himself honor, nobility, and importance by speaking of God as an artist." I'm perfectly aware that that accusation is there to be brought in. All I say here may indeed be no more than a projection of my own egotistical preferences.

Well, you have spoken of God as a novelist. . . .

No, I haven't. What I have said upon occasion is that God is a better novelist than the novelists—that's not the same thing.

Whether my motive is pure or impure, I do believe in God as the Artist, the Creator. That makes the most sense to me. Whether I have a private agenda, or whether I am being an objective philosopher (to the extent one can propose the existence of what may be an oxymoron—*objective* philosopher!)—

so be it. Whether guilty or innocent, this will be the argument I advance: God is an artist. And like an artist, God has successes, God has failures.

Evil, you've said more than once, is growing in power—especially in the last hundred years.

Yes.

Do you think there was ever a time in the past, a golden age, when good was in the ascendancy?

Let's say that in my lifetime, certain things have gotten better and other things have grown *worse*, so much so that latter-day events would stagger the imagination of the nineteenth century. If, for example, the flush toilet is an improvement in existence—and you can advance arguments against it, which I won't get into—but if it is an improvement, if the automobile is an improvement, again, huge arguments, if technological progress is an improvement, then look at the price that was paid. It's not too hard to argue that the gulags, the concentration camps, the atom bomb, came out of technological improvement. For the average person in the average developed country, life, if seen in terms of comfort, is better than it was in the middle of the nineteenth century, but by the measure of our human development as ethical, spiritual, responsible, and creative human beings, it may be worse.

I can't speak for other languages, but I do know the English language has hardly been improved in the last half century. Young, bright children no longer speak well; the literary artists of fifty and one hundred years ago are, on balance, superior to the literary artists of today. The philosophers have virtually disappeared—at least, those philosophers who make a difference.

I take it that, in your view of history, the Enlightenment and the rise of science were not steps forward.

Mixed steps forward. Forward and retrograde. It all depends on what God intended. I could give you a speculation—a rank speculation: Perhaps God intended that human beings would get to the point where they could communicate telepathically. To the degree that a man or woman wished to reach others in small or large numbers, he or she could transmit thoughts to them. One could create operas in one's mind, if one were musically talented, and beam them out to all who were willing to listen. All the means and modes we have of modern communication may be substitutes, ugly technological substitutes, for what was potentially there.

If you ask the average person, myself certainly included, "How do we see the image on television? How does it work?"—it's a blurred mystery. Indeed, the best engineers in the world can't tell you how it happens, why waves of sound striking the auditory nerve produce specific items of hearing. No one, for instance, can tell you what light is—they're still arguing over whether it's a wave or a particle or both. My ongoing question is whether the Enlightenment was for good or for ill. To assume automatically that the Enlightenment was good means you automatically have to say, Yes, it created marvelous freedom for many people. It also created the worst abuses of communism and fascism—so much worse than the Divine

Right of Kings. It also helped to foster the subtle, insidious abuses of technology.

I've said before that technology represents less pleasure and more power. It may be that we are supposed to arrive at our deepest achievements through pleasure and pain, rather than through interruption, static, mood disruption, and traffic jams.

I can see communism as an unhappy fruit of the Enlightenment, but isn't fascism a reaction against it? The fact that it cites the blood, the blood-consciousness, all that?

One of the cheats of the Nazis was their implicit claim that they were going back to the blood when in fact they were abusing human instinct. The extermination camps were an absolute violation of any notion of blood. The Nazis were cheating people of their deaths. They informed the camp inmates they were going to have a shower. Into the chamber they all marched, took off their clothes, happy to have a shower what with all those lice inhabiting them, hoping the shower would be hot. In they went and were gassed. Their last reaction in life had to be, "You cheated me!" They died in rage and panic. That's not going back to the blood, to instinct, to preparing oneself to enter the next world. They were obliterated by their own excess of reason. They were ready to assume that even their vile guards were capable of sanitary concerns for them, the imprisoned. How wrong they were!

Reason, ultimately, looks to strip us of the notion that there is a Creator. The moment you have a society built on reason alone, then individual power begins to substitute for the concept of a Creator. What has characterized just about every social revolution is that sooner or later revolutionary leaders go to war with each other and turn cannibalistic. Only one leader is left, an absolute dictator. Once you accept the notion that there is no God, then the ultimate direction for the Left, the Right, or the corporate Center is totalitarianism.

Are you saying that the Enlightenment was a time of victory for the Devil?

I think that first we have to ask whether the relation of God, the Devil, and the human to one another is not a warring relationship among three forces who are separate yet intertwined.

Let me assume there's a Devil always present in human affairs, very much present. Why? Because the Devil is another god and wishes to preempt the god who exists. The Devil has other notions of what existence could be. I'd go so far as to assume that technology is the Devil's invention. Like God, the Devil wants to have power in the universe, whereas God wants that power to satisfy His vision of what the universe could be.

Do you ignore the presence of Christ?

Christ may well be God's son, a physical and spiritual entity whom God decided was necessary for humanity. So, yes, Jesus may have been real. If I wish to argue against revealed dogma, that doesn't mean all of it seems invalid to me. Jesus does make a kind of sense. Jesus as a principle of love, compassion, forgiveness, and mercy is something we can all comprehend. We feel it in ourselves. We feel it as the best part of ourselves, the gentlest, richest, most generous part. But organized religions repel me because of the philosophical inconsistency of their God before whom they prostrate themselves, God the Almighty, God the All-Powerful. I think that's where the philosophical trouble begins: the idea that God is All-Good and All-Powerful. The history of the twentieth century demonstrated the contradiction in those terms, and most dramatically. How can we not face up to the fact that if God is All-Powerful, He cannot be All-Good? Or She cannot be All-Good. If God is All-Good, then God is not All-Powerful. To answer this contradiction, theologians have been tying themselves into philosophical knots for the last ten centuries.

Much of your thinking seems to be premised on the event of the Holocaust. I wonder if there had never been Hitler, would your notion of a limited, embattled God have been conceived? Is Hitler the final thing that pushed you into that belief?

Since I'm Jewish, the fair answer to that is probably yes. But there still would have been the gulags. And the failure of Bolshevism. The noblest social idea to come along, the most intense and advanced form of socialism, proved to be a monstrosity. That alone would be enough. Then came a capitalist contribution—the atom bomb, the fact that one hundred thousand people could be wiped out at a stroke. And this in the early stages of nuclear development. So if you eliminate all three of those, Hitler, gulags, atom bombs, then maybe I couldn't have come to these ideas. But historically speaking, you can't perform such an excision. Those three horrors dominate the twentieth century—not to mention the trench warfare of the First World War, which, indeed, accelerated the growth of communism.

The whole problem of evil—Voltaire heard about the earthquakes in Lisbon in 1755 and said the destruction proved there was no God. Throughout our history, humans have questioned God whenever there was a disaster—of course, many of these were natural disasters. That was bad enough. But, of course, why would God allow a natural disaster? You can't blame any of that on humans. That was Voltaire's point. At least we can blame the Holocaust on human evil or the Devil—in part, at least. We can't blame an earthquake in Lisbon in which one hundred thousand people were killed—we can't blame that on human beings.

No.

So that forced many philosophical thinkers of the Enlightenment into declaring, "That's it. God can't possibly exist." But if you take a step back, you can say, Maybe we're looking at too small a scale. Yes, in the concentration camps, eleven million people were exterminated with untold suffering. The suffering was so great it's impossible for us to conceive of it. To anyone who's ever looked at the photographs or read the accounts, it's horrifying to an extreme degree. But maybe, in the larger scheme of things, God was allowing this to happen to send a message to humanity on how far we have slipped, and He was even willing to sacrifice his Chosen People, or a great number of them, in order to send a message to humanity that it was time to embrace love, compassion, justice, whatever had to be done. Strong medicine, I'm saying. More and more—the earthquake in Lisbon doesn't do it, okay, we'll have trench warfare. And then we'll have gulags, the Holocaust, then the threat of the atomic bomb. And indeed, the atomic bomb was dropped, but after all we have not had a nuclear holocaust—we backed away. Maybe we've learned, and we've backed away from the brink of a nuclear disaster and spared the world.

I think we have. It's possible that even the Devil was appalled by the bombs. Nuclear warfare could destroy all of his technology.

So maybe it worked.

Let's go back to the earthquake in Lisbon. Let me give you my notion of God as the Artist—that is, a God limited in power. For example, why are there volcanoes? I would answer: because God is not a perfect engineer. That makes as much sense to me as God punishing us and punishing us with dubious compensatory result. It's very hard to argue that these acts of nature engender more than a passing shiver of religiosity in most people.

II

God, the Devil, and Humankind

MICHAEL LENNON: *Are you ready to talk about the Devil?*

NORMAN MAILER: My notion of the Devil depends to a good degree on Milton. I think he fashioned a wonderful approximation to what the likelihood might be. In one way or another, there was a profound argument between God and some very high angels—or between God and gods—and the result was finally that one god won, the God we speak of as our Creator. God won, but it was a Pyrrhic victory, because Lucifer, if you will, also became well installed. And this war has gone on ever since, gone on in us.

Whatever the form this takes, my understanding is that God and the Devil are often present in our actions. As I've said many times over the years, when we work with great energy it's because our best motive and our worst motive—or to put it another way, God and the Devil—are equally engaged in the outcome and so, for a period, working within us. There can be collaboration between opposites, as well as war. This collaboration can consist of certain agreements—"The rules of war will be. . . ." And of course, the rules can be broken. The Devil can betray God. Once in a while, God also breaks the rules—with a miracle. But my argument is that when we act with great energy, it is because God and the Devil have the same interest in the outcome. (Their differences will be settled later.) Whereas when we work with little energy, it's because They are not only at odds but are countermanding each other's impact upon us.

What if God happens to be dominating us? Wouldn't that be better? Couldn't we argue that it would be better to have God motivating us more than the Devil? Many heroes in history have been so motivated and have gone on to achieve great things. Like Constantine—"in this sign, conquer, in hoc signo, vinces!"—and goes on to—

Claim, if you wish, that Constantine was a mighty king who helped Christianity to triumph—indeed, he did. You could also say he may have helped to destroy something more fertile than Christianity, which was the richness of pagan belief. Our latter-day troubles might have started in the instant that Constantine decided to become a Christian.

Let me put it this way: If schizophrenia is on the rise—I don't know that it is—but if it is on the rise in human affairs—

—I'd be surprised if it weren't.

All right, would that be an indication that this suggested collaboration between God and the Devil is not working well?

Let's not emphasize "collaboration." I've spoken of it as "the accepted rules of the game." Take an average contest in professional football. Two teams fight each other on the field with skill and bestiality, each side laboring to win. Nonetheless, a whole set of laws also prevails. After they tackle a guy, they don't kick him in the head. I'm saying that in order to keep it flowing, God and the Devil have certain understandings with each other. What they are, I couldn't begin to say. We don't often come close to the nature of divine mysteries, but sometimes we can obtain some sense of which relations are involved. The only clue I have is that when there is great energy available to us—then I do expect They are in a temporary collaboration.

But generally speaking, we are mired in good and evil— mired because we spend most of our time in trade-offs and in the exhaustion of our efforts. One part of us wants to do something to which the other part is opposed.

Very often within us, good fights an offensive battle against evil. We know that. The Christian churches are built on that: Fight the evil in your soul.

Saint Michael the Archangel.

Yes. But my argument is that it has become a contest among three protagonists. It isn't that we are passive onlookers while God and the Devil wage a war within us. We are the third force and don't always know which side we are on in any given moment, or whether on another occasion we are independent of both.

If you'll accept my notion that technology may be the most advanced, extreme, and brilliant creation of the Devil— for technology, of course, does incredible things—then you get a real sense of why some people would be more leagued with the Devil than devoted to God. Half the human universe must by now be on the side of technology.

Let me push your idea a little further. You are saying that when you have the most energy, when you're moving forward, it is because your good and your bad motives are in sync—wouldn't that argue, then, that when everyone felt like that more and more, and we had this great sense of energy, that we're moving forward, accomplishing positive results, happiness results—

—war also results. It's not simple. Powerful energies can arouse opposition. USA versus USSR. I would also say that it is ennobling to face existence with the recognition that you are not going to have clear answers. At best, you can arrive at hypotheses that you can test—most imperfectly—by the ongoing experiences of your life.

The Manichaeans did see God and the Devil as brothers who fight until the end of time, but at the end good will defeat evil. Is that where you depart from the Manichaeans?

Absolutely. We don't know the end—we could end with the failure of the good. Because if the good is guaranteed to win at the end, then we are engaged in a wrestling match, a fixed one. If goodness is assured an ultimate victory over evil, we are in a comedy, and I must say it is an ugly farce, considering how we suffer in the course of the contest.

Go back to football—no football team ever assumes it is written they will win a big game. A victory brings the joy that it was *not* predetermined in advance—it was achieved. I'm saying existence consists of a continuing set of achievements and defeats.

Forever and ever?

No, but certainly up to the point where humankind enters into some definitive metamorphosis of existence, arriving perhaps at the notion that God is not the most powerful deity in the universe—but can succeed, nonetheless, in promulgating His vision into other worlds and other gods. It may be that our vision can join eventually with God's vision. Perhaps our mission is to travel out across the stars—not necessarily in spaceships but by our spirits ready to seek to make a better universe. But, of course, we can certainly fail. Who knows what other forces are out there in the galaxies? Dare I mention black holes in space? But enough! I don't want to stray too far from the speculations already presented.

Let me take up the "Four Last Things" of Christian eschatology: death, judgment, Heaven, Hell. You have commented, at least obliquely, on all but one, Heaven. Why have you given Heaven such short shrift?

Because I don't believe in it.

Without a vision of Heaven, your belief system is unlikely to draw many adherents.

I'm not trying to found a religion. I think if these ideas of mine have any value, a great deal of time will go by before there are any adherents. First of all, however, I believe that our childlike notion of Heaven has to be relinquished.

But not Hell?

I don't believe in absolute Hell any more than I believe in Heaven, certainly not in Hell as a place of eternal punishment. It strikes me as prodigiously wasteful.

You set the play you made out of your novel The Deer Park *in Hell. Hell is something you refer to all the time. It's a constant reference. But Heaven is absent.*

It was perfectly legitimate, I felt, to put my characters in Hell because Hell is a point of reference for everyone. Everyone believes in Hell—and much more readily than we do in Heaven. Heaven is harder to conceive of. What we all know is that the most perfect moments in our lives don't last for long. Extraordinary moments are perishable. Whereas we can be in Hell for months, even years; we can live in towering depression. Hell, therefore, is much more available to human beings as a set of stages. It was easy for me to situate the play of *The Deer Park* in Hell. It gave a foundation to the drama.

Yet I still don't believe in Hell as eternal punishment. Rather, Hell has dimensions. Some parts of it are critically worse than others. We can approach that when we talk about reincarnation. My notion remains that the only Heaven and Hell we ever receive—the only judgment that comes to us—

is by way of reincarnation. To wit, as a reward we can be given a better possibility in our next life. Or we can be born into a worse one, if that is what we deserve.

In other words, I'm not interested in absolute moral judgments, eternal Heaven, eternal Hell—to the contrary. Just think of what it means to be a good man or a bad one. What, after all, is the measure of difference? The good guy may be 65 percent good and 35 percent bad—that's a *very* good guy. The average decent fellow might be 54 percent good, 46 percent bad—and the average mean spirit is the reverse. So say I'm 60 percent bad and 40 percent good—for that, must I suffer eternal punishment?

The argument I would advance is that Heaven and Hell make no sense if the majority of humans are a complex mixture of good and evil. There's no reason to receive a reward if you're 57/43—why sit around forever in an elevated version of Club Med? That's almost impossible to contemplate. You remember the fun George Bernard Shaw had with his expectation of Heaven as a prodigiously boring place where Don Juan nonetheless wished to reside because at least you could think there? That was the best Shaw could come up with as a concept for Heaven—at least you can think well and carefully.

Now, there are Catholic theologians, including my good friend Eugene Kennedy, who write of the upper reaches of Heaven, where the best of humans refine their souls as they come to comprehend more and more of the majesty and exceptional subtlety of the Godhead. It is beautifully stated, but to my critical spirit does not answer one fundamental question, to wit: What is the end of such illumination? Its sole purpose still seems to offer no more than a further understanding of the love of God and the great importance that we love Him more and more.

There is no suggestion that the Lord might have greater needs than His or Her own glorification. The point to all my suppositions is that God still has an unfulfilled vision and wishes to do more. So I would suppose that we receive instead a partial reward or partial punishment and it is meted out to us in our reincarnation. How better to account for the ongoing feeling of conscience that we all seem to have? Conscience is there for good cause; conscience is vital—if, for nothing else, it's there because it gives us a clue to what is likely to be our next future. Will we be reborn in a situation that offers more opportunities? Or, for punishment, will there be fewer good chances? Will our next life be easier or more painful?

Now, this notion is simple, but people who are fixed entirely on notions of eternal Hell and eternal Heaven can't come near to it. They cannot comprehend what I'm talking about. Yet for those who are wondering if there is a viable scheme to the afterlife, these assumptions can become meaningful. Why do I strive to become a better person? Can it be because I wish to have a somewhat better life the next time out? If I am going to be reborn, I want to be able to do more in my next incarnation than with this last one.

I have a joke to tell at this point: I die and go up before the Monitoring Angel. He says, "Oh, Mr. Mailer, we're so glad to see you. We've been waiting. Now, tell us—we ask everyone this—what would be your idea of a proper reincarnation for yourself? What would you like to be in your next life?"

I say, "Well, you know, everything considered, I think I'd like to be a black athlete. I won't argue with where you position me at birth—it can be under poor, ugly circumstances, I'm willing to take that on—but I would like to be a black athlete."

The Monitor's face clouds up. "Oh, Mr. Mailer," he says, "everyone these days wants to be a black athlete. Right now, we're dreadfully oversubscribed. So let me see where you have been put." He looks it up. He says, "I'm afraid we've got you down for cockroach. But—here is the good news—you'll be the fastest cockroach on the block!"

All right—we are going to be reincarnated. Whether we know what our reincarnation will be, I doubt. I expect it will be full of surprises, most unforeseen. Some, given our vanity, are likely to seem outrageously warped.

Whenever you've spoken of reincarnation, you've done so in an ironic manner. You talk about directives in the Bureau of Karmic Reassignment. But I don't recall your ever talking about the likelihood of the reassignments. In your mind, how does reincarnation work? Who controls the process?

God.

Let me try to engage these unverifiable concepts. Does this tie in to God's need for humans to be soldiers in His future cosmic war? Is it an operation run altogether by God? Are all souls recycled? Are new ones created?

Let me work through your questions one by one. First, I would assume that God has ultimate hegemony. I am sure there are any number of monitoring angels. It's a bureaucracy, if you will. We don't have to be precise about it. Where did our human bureaucracy come from? I feel many of our social forms derive from celestial forms. In other words, bureaucracies could be human representations of the notion of how it might work—and not work—in the heavens. We can't stand bureaucracy because of the boredom, repetition, and slowness. But it may be that there are also elements in Heaven that do not work with high efficiency even when there are angels at the switchboard rather than humans.

You did remark that not all souls are recycled.

I believe the soul is a gift from God. Of course, you can abuse any living gift. Any number of people may end by saying, "All I want is a little peace. Let me sleep forever." They may be given just that.

So such a termination is not necessarily a function of evil. . . .

Not necessarily of evil—but it is giving up. If the complications of life and the exhaustion of contending with all the little gods and devils in yourself burn you out, there can come a point where the soul loses its desire to exist. You see, reincarnation is a gamble. You could do worse the next time. Fear of an even more painful existence may convince you to throw in your hand. Or God could so decide for you. On the other hand, I think there are humans who choose to commit physical suicide because they feel that if they don't their souls will die before their bodies. Gary Gilmore was a perfect example. Why did he so desire to be executed? Because he expected his soul would expire in prison, and he was a great believer in the value of his own ongoing soul.

You are saying that a soul doesn't necessarily go to Heaven or to Hell—it just ceases to exist.

Yes. It's gone. It's in a true cemetery.

Are new souls being created?

I don't talk much to people who believe in reincarnation because I don't like the jargon. But, yes, people who believe in reincarnation do speak of new souls or "young souls"— and, yes, I would expect God creates new spiritual lives. God may say, "I've been reconsidering the terrible propensities of the Devil. Let us see if we can conceive of a soul who will be able to war with the Devil a little more effectively, a new soul who will have many of the qualities of the Devil but can transmute them, transform them, elevate our sense of spirit even in the dirtiest, ugliest, foulest places. We can call on Dostoyevsky at this point. God may have decided that an iota of goodness in an evil soul can be immensely important.

You hardly speak of the casualties in this war between God and the Devil.

While the soul is presumably a separate being from the body, I would suppose that the soul also has its period of existence. A particular soul might expire after a single earthly existence, another could be reincarnated a number of times, but doubtless there's a limit. Yes, souls do expire, I must suppose. Just as God may finally expire, or the Devil, indeed. There are forces out there who wouldn't mind seeing the collapse of one, the other, or both. We may be speaking of a force that consists of the drive to nothingness. Nothingness may be a huge power out in the great cosmic universe. It may desire the extinction of the universe. To repeat: We have yet to explain black holes in space. What in the nature of things accounts for that exceptional megaconcentration of gravitational forces that pulls all nearby matter into it?

You've always said you are on the side of being.

Yes, but it's like saying, "I'm a Yale man," or "Loyal to Harvard." The built-in pitfall of these conversations is how to keep from sounding sententious at one end and hollow at the other. Theological remarks tend to be pious and/or presumptuous. Nevertheless, I take this route because I am weary of the philosophical paradoxes and evasions that good Christians tie themselves up in, those mutually exclusive conundrums. "God's ways are mysterious" can be a cop-out. Resolutely, they evade any reply that can explore down to the root. The set of beliefs offered here makes sense at least to me. And I would add: Having a view of the universe that makes sense to oneself is, I think, Jung's finest prescription for mental health. One of his conclusions was that nobody could be cured of their neurosis until they found their own vision of God. That may be a profound, even a fabulous idea. I believed it before I could articulate it, so I was naturally excited when I came across that set of remarks in his work.

Many people who believe in reincarnation would say they have re-
tained some sense of their previous life. You've always said that you
don't remember.

My feeling is there's a very good reason why not—I believe there's a psychic wall within us that shuts off recollec-
tions of any previous existence. Think what your life would
be if you knew about three or four previous spent and mis-
spent lives. My memory is already failing for the one life I'm
aware of. How could I handle the confusion of other existences that were also mine? I do think, however, that we retain deep instincts about previous incarnations. Sometimes
we have reactions to events that are inexplicable. Something
inside says, "Don't take another step in this direction." Or "I
will pursue this course even if it makes no sense to me whatsoever." Some people are maniacs on motorcycles—what do
they get from it? Something not ordinary. Partly from this
life—they're curing hostilities, aggressions, and rages they
can only solve on a motorcycle that is going fast on a wet
road. But maybe it also derives from a previous life when they
were terrified of any commitment to danger. Perhaps the soul
is now turning over the soil of previous arid endeavors.

So many people who believe in reincarnation have self-aggrandizing
memories of the past—"Oh, I was in Cleopatra's court."

I can't bear that.

It kind of put me off reincarnation.

Yes, that particular vanity is atrocious. It's unpleasant in
the same manner that people who are devout Christians be-

lieve they're going to Heaven because they're steadfast in
their belief. Either way, it is self-aggrandizement.

At the end of Ancient Evenings, *which I've been rereading over
the last few days, Meni the Second, the young Meni, says, "Purity
and goodness are less to Osiris than strength," which is a restate-
ment of what Cherry says in* An American Dream: *"God is
weaker because I didn't turn out well." Add to that Rojack's belief
that "God was not love but courage. Love came only as a reward."
You return to this idea many times in your books—especially in*
Harlot's Ghost. *I can see the force of this idea, but couldn't it be
argued that love can create strength just as courage generates love?*

Yes, it can be argued. It is still a question, however. Does
love have as powerful and vital an effect as courage? There
are any number of men and women who are full of love but
are nonetheless timid and cowardly and hate themselves for
being cowardly—it poisons the love in them, even if, essentially, they are loving creatures.

*In Christian belief, love can move mountains. But for you, love
seems to be more of a passive quality, not active like courage—love
comes as a "reward"—so it isn't seen as an active principle. It's the
emolument you get for being courageous.*

Let me tell you how I got to that point. It struck me that
everyone I knew, including myself, was always looking for
love. "Ah, if I could find love, it would solve my problems."
Some years ago, however, I found myself saying to my children, "Don't go searching for love. Love is not a solution but

a reward." So long as you go searching for love directly, you will fail. Because love is a grace, and you don't pursue grace. Now, mind you, I'm not a macho maniac on courage. More than once I've said that an old lady who crosses a busy street in terror, feeling she hardly has a fifty-fifty chance of making it safely across, is exhibiting courage that might be more intense than that of a professional soldier attacking a machine-gun nest, if through all his young manhood he's been ready to die in such an action. Odds are that such a soldier is braver even on balance than the average old lady, but we can't set up a hierarchy concerning courage.

Still, my own experience tells me that to the degree one is brave, one finds more love than when one is cowardly.

But I'm not talking about romantic love, rather about what Christianity calls "charity."

Charity comes when you're brave. How many cowards are full of charity? Cowardice is a poison.

It's a question of precedence. You always put courage as the more active, the more powerful—

I often find when I'm feeling weak that I'm also very nice, and when I'm weak I feel the weakness in others and am sympathetic to it. But it's not nourishing. It can be just another form of emptiness traveling back and forth. Whereas when I'm feeling strong and also feel compassion or charity—on those rare occasions—there's real goodness present. It's of real use to the other person.

Well, to get down to basic ethics: When someone does something that's an act of real generosity done at a cost to themselves, it's because they love the other person. I don't mean in a romantic or sexual way.

I'm not putting that down, but I'm not ready to elevate it—because as a novelist, I know better. Forgive me for putting it this way, but most often when you have an act of great generosity, there's a tangled skein behind it of good and bad motive—not to ignore the possible presence of God and the Devil. Contemplate the compromises, relations, treaties, surprises, and rebellions within any large personal act. People are also perfectly capable of rebelling against both God and the Devil, shutting them both out of one's existence as far as possible. There is the human ego—the notion that neither God nor the Devil knows what He now wants of me as well as I know it. So I do call it a tripartite relationship, and by that I certainly don't mean that humans are subservient in it. What terrifies me at times is that humans may become dominant over the other two. I just don't trust us to go traveling across the universe on our own.

You mean there may have been some individuals in history who were so powerful at a certain moment in time, they equaled God and the Devil? Churchill, Napoleon—

—Napoleon, yeah. I think certain humans can free themselves to the point where both God and the Devil are working for them for a brief period. But, please, take us back again to speculations I feel closer to.

You've eliminated Heaven and Hell from the Four Last Things.

As absolutes. But Hell can be very real—take some proud society lady who is unpleasant to her servants. She is all caught up in money and her jewels—we all know people like that. She's willing to sell herself to the Devil, but even the Devil rejects her because, at bottom, she's a silly ass. He doesn't need her. So there she is, ready for judgment, and God's judgment is: "You'll be a scrubwoman in your next existence. And if you complain once, you'll clean latrines—provided you still have any soul left."

Most conservatives believe that the poor man has as good a chance or better of getting to Heaven as the rich man because the temptations among the rich are so awful that they can easily go to Hell. And that's what enables conservatives to function. They can put up with inequity for others in this life because they feel there's a better existence waiting for those poor who are patient and good in horrible circumstances.

Well, I believe there's an element of truth in that, just as there's an element of truth in the implicit liberal faith that every soul, every human, is terribly important and must be protected in this life. These are not only warring notions but may be warring notions within God. Because where is the artist who does not have such profound disputes within? The Creation may have come out of these warring notions in the Creator.

It isn't that God is only fighting the Devil. He's also debating within Himself or Herself what the next proper course might be. I wish to suggest that it is in experiencing the play of this complexity that future theology could find its nourishment rather than in the churchly insistence that God's final intentions are all in the Book. No, I do not see the laws of existence as etched in stone, with no deviation permitted. No absolute Heaven or absolute Hell. Such concepts are devilish ways to confuse ourselves thoroughly, because they don't add up. In terms of our experience, they don't make much sense. Our experience is that everything in life is more or less shaded. On certain days, certain things are better; certain of our acts give us more pleasure than on others.

Sometimes evil acts—what we see as evil acts if we believe in Revelation—give us pleasure that we find ungodly, devilish. Yet acts that we think are evil may have been inspired by God, who decides, "This poor wretch is going to expire unless there's a breakout. This poor soul has to do something unpleasant before it can feel any life again." In this sense, God's compassion can also be present in an ugly or even an evil act.

Never forget Frederick Engels's immortal three words: "Quantity changes quality." Petty evil is one thing. Massive evil is another. I'd never use an argument like this to arrive at a justification of Hitler or Stalin. They embodied massive evil.

Considering your belief in various states of grace and the idea of dying in a state of grace, it seems to me that if there's any pathway to formal religion open in your mind, it's to Catholicism.

I probably do feel more connection to elements of Catholicism than to any of the other formal religions. But that's as far as it goes. I was talking once with a Catholic theologian who said, "Well, so much of what you say seems Catholic."

I said, "Yes, but I could never be a Catholic."

He asked, "Why? Would it be the transubstantiation in the Mass?"

I said, "No. I could believe that. Why can't God be present in a wafer? That would not bother me. Why can't wine become the blood of Christ? I wouldn't believe it in a hurry, but that wouldn't keep me from becoming a Catholic."

So we went through various hurdles and obstacles, and finally he asked again, "Why, then, can't you be a Catholic?"

"Because," I said, "I don't believe in the omnipotence of God."

And he said, "In that case, I can understand why you're not a Catholic."

All right. Let's return one more time to reincarnation. I feel that you have more to say on that.

Yes. One matter we've not gotten into is my supposition that the atom bomb, the concentration camps, and the gulags were mighty efforts by the Devil to foul up reincarnation, to choke off the subtlety of the divine judgment within reincarnation. I hope I've suggested the delicate dispositions of God, the care with which the question is asked: "What shall I do with this soul?" That is at the core of reincarnation—delicate, responsible, artful, *deliberate* judgment. If the process is overloaded, it can break down.

So mass slaughter fouls up the divine bureaucracy?

Contemplate the mess in eternity when so many human creatures were being slaughtered at once and en masse.

Not if you can go back to an omnipotent God. Most people believe God can handle anything and everything

No, God's energies are also limited. Everything I say is based on such a premise. We may live in a universe that is expanding, but there is not always endless energy available. No. No.

Are you saying that the Devil does have a purchase on the process of reincarnation?

Through marring it, mainly. Or overloading it.

It was Herman Melville who said—in a line I could never forget—when he was, if I recall, writing Moby-Dick. *He said, "Lord, when shall we stop growing?" In your theological belief, there's a paradox, to me at least, in that on the one hand, growth is something you're always seeking, and it is the summum bonum—*

Not all growth is good.

But good growth is good, positive growth; growth of some kind is better than stasis.

Good growth is good; bad growth is bad. The growth of suburban shopping malls has been prodigious in America—does that mean it's good? Does it mean that, because the old family store gave way to the corporate chain, the family store was inferior? Not necessarily. Not humanly.

Let me ask you about evolution. You accept evolution. You know, the traditional Catholic belief here—the Catholics were quick to embrace evolution even as many Protestants, at least Fundamentalist Protestants, were not. The Catholics were among the earliest to embrace the notion of evolution, and they didn't have any trouble with it. They said, People coming from monkeys—no trouble at all, that's how the body was created. And at a certain point, God put the soul in. Is that . . .

I happen to believe that dogs have souls.

Well . . .

Mind you, in reincarnation, you may not come back as a human. You could come back as a dog, and, I will say in parentheses, that makes a great deal of sense to me, because so many dogs, I find, are closer to the human than humans.

Stretch evolution back—people from monkeys or dogs is no trouble at all. That's just three million years. But going back—fifty, sixty, one hundred million years—when the creatures were coming out of the slime, do you see that at a certain point God puts—

I don't think it's answerable—even as speculation.

Well, what doesn't have a soul?

It makes more sense for me to believe that God was in the slime from the beginning, and God was less in those days. God has grown with us. God has grown with evolution.

Well, God created the world—

God may have been developing along with evolution. Why must a god be independent of time?

Well, if God created the world at that point, He wasn't slime.

Wait: We create our children. That doesn't mean one is able to create children on the day one is born. I'm not talking about an omnipotent, All-Powerful God but one who grows with us.

I'm assuming that in the course of human history, God at some point began the process of creating souls.

These souls also developed. The soul of an amoeba would be primitive but still a soul that gave the amoeba some intimation of direction, some sense that it must do its best under its own limited circumstances. God, doubtless, was superior to the amoeba from the beginning, but God was also developing even as the Creation went from the amoeba to the paramecium to the multicelled creature.

Here's where I have a problem with your notion of reincarnation—when did God create such a process?

It may have occurred only after God endowed a great many higher animals and humans with souls. He may then have decided, "I, as an artist, can improve on this Creation. Some could have turned out better if they had not lived their lives under grievous circumstances. Give them, therefore, another opportunity to exercise their free will. Maybe they will be wiser." It comes down to something basic. God's notion: Let's make the Creation better. The Devil's: Let's maim the Creation. I have, says the Devil, something in mind that will supplant and replace it.

What would the Devil want? Total destruction? Nihilism?

For the sake of argument, let's say the Devil would want to fashion a universe on His or Her terms.

Have we any idea what those terms would be?

I suppose it could be an immensely technological universe where the need for existence—individual existence—and the concomitant need for soul would be less. That might be more to the Devil's taste: individual units functioning in relation to other individual units. Less spiritual. More mechanized. That seems to be the prevailing tendency in the twentieth and early twenty-first centuries—more and more interchangeable units, ready to serve a corporate machine. At the other end of it, you have the maniacal intensity of the most extreme Muslims, whose only feeling is that there's something so wrong with this approach that it all has to be destroyed, and don't ask questions. Once again, we are at a point in history between the rock and the hard place.

III

Purgatory, Heaven, and Hell

MICHAEL LENNON: *I want to ask a question about Purgatory. Do you feel some sympathy for that idea?*

NORMAN MAILER: Some—and a fair portion of uneasiness. I will say that I expect there may be some sizable difficulties present after death, a universal Hell, perhaps, of waiting that we may all have to go through before we are born again— those of us who will be born again. I will add that there's an automatic assumption in most people who are religious that God is not only All-Powerful but instantaneous in His action. There's an Irish saying: "When God made time, He made a lot of it." So God *could* be instantaneous—but why would He want to be? Nevertheless, this expectation of quick reception and quick designation for one's afterlife is at odds with our own experience—which is that everything takes longer than we think it will. That is the accrued wisdom of most men and women after many decades of life. In the economy of human experience, there are always time-consuming episodes you didn't anticipate. To assume that once you pass into another realm of existence things will be faster and more responsive— that is no small assumption. It's as ungrounded as to expect that there are no destinations in the Hereafter other than Purgatory, Limbo, or Hell. Another, after all, might be God's need to judge whether a particular soul should be reborn or might as well expire. So Purgatory might sit there as a set of possibilities with many unhappy holding tanks. God may look at three quarters of us, say, "I don't want to make up my mind just yet," and drop us into slow Purgatory, so to speak.

Now, what the form of this Purgatory might be—whether it bears resemblance to a Palestinian refugee camp—I have no idea. One of the beliefs I hold is that the Hereafter is less different than we assume. We may have the same frustrations and difficulties in the afterlife—overcrowding, for example, or even, conceivably, waste. After the Holocaust, we were forced to recognize there was something absolutely murderous in our species—obviously, it was not just reserved for the Germans; there was something vastly destructive in our nature. We received this knowledge over and over again, in Russia, in China, in Africa, in some of our own actions— indeed, in Vietnam. The point I want to make is that the Holocaust may have exacted a great price from God, even greater than from us. At the core of karma is the notion that it is composed of wise judgment. What if that is not always true? In the godly assessment of each life—in the reading of the soul, so to speak, that takes place after one dies—can it be that God sometimes says, "I'm too weary to think about this now"? After all, if God is an artist, is it always necessary to make instantaneous judgments? Under certain conditions of overcrowding, literal overcrowding in eternity of the sort caused by the Holocaust or Hiroshima, Purgatory can become a vast way station.

Let me try to expatiate on that. Given the number of people exterminated in a day during the Holocaust, the number of souls arriving in tumult, is it possible they became too great in number for God to measure with calm and justice? It may be that karma has been in a species of uproar ever since the Holocaust, the atom bomb, and the gulags.

The moment you postulate that God is striving to promulgate His vision across the stars, you are also postulating that the nature of the Beyond—to use another word than the Hereafter—is existential. Not fixed, but changing with cosmic circumstances.

Well, you have certainly touched on my next question. You see God as an artist. I think all too often your visions of the Hereafter or the Beyond are built on your own experience of this life. Couldn't God just as well be an engineer?

Absolutely.

Or a general?

Yes.

A public administrator? Or a diplomat?

Yes, yes.

Those are all human occupations.

How can God not be all those things? God is certainly an engineer. An engineer would see it all in terms of future construction. How do you organize the Hereafter? How do you arrive at the best levels of spiritual sanitation? Yes! Heavenly comfort stations for psychic waste are not necessarily to be taken for granted. When I speak of God as an artist, I don't pretend to mean that God might be a novelist, as if that is all God is up to. Finally, the word "artist" has hegemony over other professions because whatever else, it is creative. God is a creator. A Creator. I don't like the prefix "mega"—it's been used too often—but God is, all right, at the least, a mega-artist. All the faculties of engineering, war, social building, art, music, sport, painting, science, philosophy, medicine, herbology are His or Hers, and at a level more highly developed than we can begin to conceive. But God is still an artist. A great engineer is an artist. So is a great general like Clausewitz or Robert E. Lee. So are the best in all human categories. We point to that in our own speech. We do speak of artists at war. That is the sense in which I want to use the word. I don't want to diminish this projection of what God might be. Let's think of the size of the Creation. Even if God is not All-Powerful, we have only to contemplate the vast extent of flora and fauna, the painterly touches—to offer one example—revealed in the chromatic scales of a butterfly's wing.

Well, the thing that did appeal to me about your notion of God as an artist—and, indeed, as a novelist—is that novelists have to conceive of the destinies and the forked paths that people take through their lives and so create the second phase, the third phase. In a sense, that's very much like God presiding over reincarnation— the second, third, fourth phases. God as an artist is portraying His or Her conception of the metamorphoses in each character's destiny.

Well, we are parts of God's vision, certainly. I believe that, yes—lively but seriously skewed parts of God's vision. That, I would add quickly, is because the Devil is also present. I don't presume to say exactly what part He plays in cosmic affairs or local earthly matters—but in any event, we are not pure representations of God. We are tainted, warped, even treacherous in relation to the divine projects offered us. We are torn between God and the Devil, and our own vanity can be counter to both of them. Across the centuries, human vanity has become a factor, a prodigious factor. The human ego, which has always been fearful of God's power and the Devil's—that same human ego can still separate itself into a simulacrum of omnipotent confidence. There's nothing more irritating to most of us than the feeling that we are not completely under our own power, that other forces are pushing us, external forces that are stronger than we are: "Oh, God, here comes that awful compulsion starting up again," whatever it is—some impulse we consider unworthy of ourselves or too risky for our adventurous capacities or opposed too magnetically to our spiritual inclinations.

In Advertisements for Myself, *you take sides. You say that humankind is roughly more good than evil.*

No. That was my assumption about the faith some of us have in democracy, our belief that it will work because there's more good than bad in us as a human multitude. That still remains to be proven.

Still, if we are roughly more good than evil, wouldn't that signal the ultimate victory of good?

There is no guarantee. This is an existential question—which is to say, a not-yet-determined answer. To say "existential" means you are in the midst of an activity to which you cannot see the result. Rather, you are living in the midst of an intense question. I think existentialism can only be understood in that manner.

It becomes more and more clear to me all the time why courage must be the cardinal virtue in your cosmic scheme. If the forces of good are brave, strong, and daring, then there's a chance that evil will be defeated. Would the pacifism of a Gandhi or a Martin Luther King play into the Devil's hands, then? Would He applaud its use?

Everything plays into the Devil's hands. We live in an immensely complicated mesh of cause and effect. I can make an argument for Gandhi and against him—that's no problem. One can also take either side for some great general: pro-Napoleon, let's say, or anti-Napoleon. Gandhi, finally, was a man of significant courage. He did something no one else had ever done before. So in that sense, he was searching for the answer to the same question I'm searching for, but at a much higher and much more dangerous level: Are we more good than bad?

In India, the answer that came back to him before he died was that we may be more bad than good. The immense riots as he came to power—those events had to be a spiritual disaster for him. So I certainly don't sneer at Gandhi, nor would I wish to systematize him by declaring, "Oh, he brought on so much that was bad because he advocated passivity." After all, his kind of passivity demanded huge courage. And discipline. Heroic passivity. One of the things we might do well to begin to try to understand as humans will be our future need to reconstruct the essential energy contained in oxymorons. Certain oxymorons are absurdities—so many, indeed, that we feel free to dismiss all of them by saying, "It's an oxymoron." But there are a few that are vital and valuable. One of them is "heroic passivity." There, one's experience must serve as the arbiter. There can be heroic passivity, or quasi-heroic passivity. The latter can be a disaster. And we've all seen that: stubborn, frantic passivity—certain pacifists we'd like to throw down the stairs.

What came first in your scheme of things? Belief in courage as the cardinal virtue? Or does your vision of the divided universe require courage to be the cardinal virtue?

I would rather go back to God's experience as He or She was creating the flora and fauna of existence, all those incredible biological experiments that went on over millions of

years. Plus, most crucially, the percipience gathered from the
failures. Think of the excitement of God when the dinosaur
came into being, the immense excitement that He had something pretty big and pretty formidable. Then it proved too
big—badly designed. The record of bad design in evolution is
also there, could stuff the shelves of many a library. Yet what
became obvious was that animals who had courage—or those
plants that had a kind of odd integrity, if you will, in terms
of their environment—seemed to do better for the most part
than those who didn't. Of course, there are animals—we can
see this directly—who had too much courage. This notion of
balance underwriting courage is what God began to search for.

*Let me shift a little bit over to the dark side, to the Devil. If things
are indeed getting worse—if Satan, as you seem to fear, could be
winning—why would the Devil wish to destroy the world, rather
than run the world as an ultimate tyrant? Wouldn't he wish to rule
humans, convert them to his evil slaves and minions, rather than
destroy them?*

Let's start with the Devil's point of view—the word "evil"
is not even present for him.

Evil is his good, as in Paradise Lost?

He might see it that way. It's such a blatant speculation,
let's have a little fun with it. My guess is that the Devil sees
God as incompetent. After all, the Devil is a fallen angel, that
I assume. Why? Because certain geniuses have come along
who had intimations of what our origins might be. Milton

was certainly one. I think Milton is as good a rule of thumb for approaching this matter of God and the Devil as anyone I've come across—homage to Milton. So I propose that the Devil's belief is that He or She could end up with a better world, a better form of existence, a more sophisticated, more intelligent, well-run notion of things. Now, what are the Devil's means? Well, our fear is that He could destroy the whole world in order to start over again. There, I'm out on the end of my mental belay—does the Devil have the same creative powers that God does to create animals, plants, humans, a system? Or is the Devil a parasite, essentially, upon God? That's a question I wouldn't presume to answer.

That's why I have more trouble dealing with the notion of the Devil than with that of God. It's relatively more direct to deal with the notion of God as the Creator.

But if you see the Devil as capable of defeating God, He must have equal powers.

Well, even at the highest level, there is such a matter as mindless destruction. When you can't win, you destroy the game. The spoiled kid who picks up the marbles comes in all forms. But such a kid hardly has to be the best player. If the Devil feels that He or She cannot gain those powers that are needed to form a new universe, the rage generated may be so intense that the next move is to destroy the works. Talk about rank speculation, let's suppose the Devil is treacherous and has sold His or Her birthright to some other god in the cosmos and will do His or Her best to turn over a paralyzed, inane, stupid, mainly destroyed world to someone who can build it up. The Devil could be a lieutenant, rather than a majordomo. In that case, the game starts all over again.

These notions of what the Devil might be are not nearly so comfortable as assuming that God is an imperfect creator. That makes sense to me. But the Devil could be this, that, anything—I don't know. One guess: Technology is an arm of the Devil, which I think is probably true. Still, technology could be a third force, ready to destroy both God and the Devil—man's assertion against God and the Devil.

The questions are wide-open. No way to propose answers yet, but perhaps the question will become somewhat more focused as the new century goes on. As of now, for example, I would assume technology is indeed the Devil's force. Why? I feel it viscerally. That's the best I can offer. I think of all the things I've detested for all these years, starting with plastic. It seems to me plastic is a perfect weapon in the Devil's armory, for it desensitizes human beings. Living in and with plastic, we are subtly sickened. And the Devil looks to destroy God's hope in us. Whether this effort looks to attain a world that can be taken over, or whether the Devil, to the contrary, aims to acquire a ruined world or works toward a world transferable to some other god are, I repeat, questions that obviously remain far beyond our reach right now.

So you're not sure whether the Devil is ambitious or nihilistic?

Why must you see that as contradictory? As a novelist, I would say some characters in Dostoyevsky are both nihilistic and immensely ambitious. The two go together. Frustrated ambition can turn quickly to nihilism. A rotten fruit can grow poisonous.

You seem to be in agreement with some of the other religions of the world on the role of saints.

Saints?

Do you see them as intermediaries, or do they play a larger role, a prophetic role? Do they actually see themselves as instruments of God, paralleling demons on the other side? I wonder if you could say something about saints and monsters.

Hagiography is not my strong point. I would guess, given my general hypotheses, that very few of the saints were wholly bona fide—by that I mean vastly more good than bad. I would think some of them had incredible powers. I believe many saints were perfectly capable of small miracles—that doesn't bother me a bit. I would take that for granted. There are such things as psychic powers, and they can be raised to a very high degree in certain humans.

But the idea that saints are as good as the hagiographers have made them out to be does give great pause because, finally, the Catholic Church may be the most complex and powerful and manipulative and intricate power system in history. But from what we have learned about history, we also know that most powerful people rewrite history to their own specifications. Many a saint may have been built up into much more than that saint deserved—the Church needed him or her at the moment. Nonetheless, I also subscribe to the notion that some people do represent the best and most magical elements in God. That is not a concept I would scorn. I believe there were, and are, saints. I would just approach them more critically than might a devout Catholic.

I guess I agree with you. In each period, the Church has to create saints of a certain stripe. But one thing that struck me about your scheme is your declaration that most of us don't know most of the time whether our actions are ultimately for good or for ill—or, indeed, which side we're helping, which hindering. But saints struck me as those who might have greater premonitions, greater knowledge of what was to come and what certain human actions could do to advance the cause of good. And I can see a similar faction on the side of the Devil—those who asked, "What can I do to bring down, hurt, or destroy some strength of the Lord?" In that sense, human demons would also be more aware of their mission.

Yes, saints are imbued with the fundamental belief that what they're doing is absolutely right—when it may not be. There's many a saint who might prove to be a devil on closer examination. And many a devil may have been working perversely to undermine the Devil.

I want to challenge your idea about things getting worse—with a couple of brief statistics. I chose these carefully. In 1900, the average American lived to be forty-six years old. Six percent of Americans graduated from high school. Only 14 percent of homes had a bathtub. Six percent had a telephone—the flush toilet was a rarity in 1900. And so on. Perhaps, as you have said, the level of language was higher among the intelligentsia. But the vast majority had

hardly any books in their homes. Today, a thousand books, I believe,
are published every day, worldwide.

So technology with all its drawbacks has changed everything in
our lives. I take it you would argue these are just local effects, short-
term gains, and that in the long run, despite any of these specific ad-
vances, technology is yet going to overwhelm us, even destroy us.

All the modern assumptions about progress are present in
what you just defended. But progressivism has yet to prove itself. Of course, all those things you cited have made life easier. I don't want to be a bore about this, but nuclear warfare
also came along. And we live in a more diffuse state of general
anxiety than people did in 1900. People were locked up then
in all sorts of terrors, intimations, obsessions, and paralyzing
anxieties, but it was all sort of local and particular. Now you
have general anxiety, of a very large and pervasive sort.

The argument: Did we really improve anything spiritually? For instance, were people better off when they had to
squat over a hole in the ground and so could smell their own
product? Maybe they were a little closer to themselves than
they are now. It's analogous to my argument about contracep-
tion. That always gets me into trouble. It's interesting that
women did not seem to conceive as often or as easily in the
Middle Ages. And, in that time, many of the babies died in
their first year. But the ones who survived may have been
hardier than the mass of us now. If we proceed further, we
have to get into all the complex arguments over whether
modern medicine is a blessing or a vitiator of human poten-
tiality. Because today, it is not only the strongest who survive.

Nobody will go near this argument because it's so Hitlerian. It may be that Hitler was not only the Devil's greatest achievement but also destroyed any possibility of thinking along the lines he laid out. People shrink the moment you say courage is important. They think, "Believe in that, and you'll end up a Nazi." Hitler did more than anyone to spoil the possibility of exploring our time—the world was left with no more than conservatism and progressivism. The more interesting human philosophies, like existentialism, were cut off.

To this day, people don't like existentialism. They hate the notion that their philosophical feet cannot always be placed on a familiar floor. Well, keep living in the familiar contexts, and it can prove stultifying. Liberals can be most stultifying. That dreadful remark—"It's a human life you're talking about"—as if all human lives are equal, as if no human life should ever be extinguished, this is a staple of political correctness, the fierce, unruly, and manic child of progressivism. So when you present these things, I would prefer to come back with a gentle, broad answer, to say, Yes, life is certainly more comfortable than it used to be, and there are more opportunities for most than there ever were, although, of course, they may be used in more mediocre fashion than similar opportunities a hundred years ago. But lives may also be more drenched in anxiety of a sort we can't locate, an anxiety that lives in us in such a way that we don't even have nightmares any longer—what we have are various stretches of poor sleep and uneasiness. I think we're weaker and more confused. I think we wander all over the place. We're also louder and more loutish.

You can ask yourself: Is this society better when it has every creature comfort that's been developed up to now and has a president like George W. Bush, as, say, opposed to Abraham Lincoln 140 years ago? Perhaps. Or perhaps we have less progress than we supposed.

Do you agree that many, if not most, humans have an inherent, or an imprinted or intuitive belief in God as All-Powerful? They can't think of God in any other way. Lots of people will say, "My intuitions are as good as Norman Mailer's, and I can't imagine a God who isn't All-Powerful."

Their intuitions may be more powerful than mine. Let me, however, go through my beliefs, sketchily. When I was a child, I believed in an All-Powerful God, of course. Most children do. Then there was a period when I was a fierce atheist. For many years! By now, philosophically speaking, atheism is more incomprehensible to me than the notion that there's a Creator. And to this day, if I were arguing with an atheist, I would suggest: "The burden of proof is on you. You have much more to explain about how we're here if you insist that there's nothing behind our existence."

But I would certainly never argue that Fundamentalists don't have intense feelings. They're immensely intense—too intense. I think this intensity reflects how terrifying the whole thing is to them. The horror for all too many would come down to this: If it all ends badly, we humans are also responsible. You see, the message of the All-Powerful God is, finally: "You're not responsible. Just keep your nose clean, observe ritual, and you'll be taken care of after you die."

I think Fundamentalism is a reflection of the deepest fears people have about dying. They feel that if they follow *all* the rules, they won't go to something worse. They take to Fundamentalism because it restricts the extent of their responsibility.

I remember in my play, *The Deer Park*, at the end, its hero, who is dying, says, "Where I go, I do not know. It may be for worse." And that is the secret terror that supports Fundamentalism. Police systems are built on it. The policeman's phrase "Keep your nose clean" is one more aspect of Fundamentalism. And the true believers' dependence on Revelation is also immense but for just that reason. I would go so far as to argue that Fundamentalism is one of the Devil's strongest tools: The Devil adores Fundamentalism because it keeps people from thinking. So long as people are incapable of pursuing a thought to where it leads, they can't begin to carry out God's notions. The irony is that by subscribing (they think) to God's will, they become desensitized to the sensitivities of divine will. They wall themselves out. They cannot work with God's will even if they long to.

Do you feel as negative about the revelations of other religions—Islam, Hinduism, Buddhism, Gnosticism—as you do about the revelations of Judaism and Christianity?

I'm less familiar with them, so I feel less negative. But I still feel suspicious. If I were a serious theologian, I would devote my years right now to studying the Koran and reading up on Buddhism, but I don't, because there are other things I wish to do with the remaining years. Still, my suspicion is great that I would find the Koran as difficult to live with as the Old and New Testaments.

With Buddhism, it's another matter entirely. That's the opposite of Fundamentalism. It's a trackless universe, which I don't pretend to understand. I get irritated sometimes by Buddhists saying, "Well, you're very much a Buddhist, whether you know it or not." And I don't know what they're talking about.

I think you're really a Gnostic.

That has no meaning for me either. But let's get into it, at least in passing. I've been called a Manichaean, a Gnostic. I am certainly not a Manichaean, because I don't believe there's necessarily a happy ending built into the endgame.

It's the Zoroastrians who really believe that. The Manichaeans believe good will win, but it won't be a total victory. They believe that evil will have stolen some of the light.

I can go along with that. I can't believe in a total victory.

Well, what happens if God does win? Suppose the Devil is totally vanquished.

God, at that point, after such a war, has been seriously wounded. And whatever happens, whatever goes on, it's not going to be God, fully resplendent, awaiting us in Heaven.

That makes you close to Manichaeanism. Evil loses, but evil takes a considerable amount of good with it as it goes under.

I can believe that. Once again, I will say, I'm a novelist. We tend to think that way. Nothing is 100 percent. The point of writing novels is to show what the costs are in human activities. If I may quote myself again, at the end of *The Deer Park*, Charles Eitel is asked by a former wife, "Do you know you have real dignity now?" "It was a decent compliment," Eitel thought, "for what was dignity, real dignity, but the knowledge written on one's face of the cost of every human desire." I've always liked that line because for me it's the essence of the novel, the frightful cost of human desire.

So why not extend that to the frightful cost of divine desire, where the loss is greater? God might have had an earlier conception of human existence more beautiful, much more beautiful than the one He's left with now.

Let me give you another model. A friend of mine has been sending me stuff on Simone Weil. I don't know if you—

I know her work slightly. Dwight Macdonald used to write about her with adoration in the years right after World War II.

Well, she's not afraid to think in bold terms—but I don't know if you'll agree. Here's one of her ideas: She believes that God became limited in the course of creating the universe. She saw the act of creating the universe as an act of renunciation, one of power sharing with humans.

I accept the power sharing; that's implicit in everything I've said.

Before that, God existed alone in His endless powers. Then suddenly He created something—He gave something away. Weil believed that humans had a role to play because of this power sharing, as did

the Devil, who profited immensely by God's creative act. She's say-
ing that God lost by doing this.

God lost, and God gained. In creating us, God acquired knowledge that could not have been obtained otherwise. So it's not just that God lost. That gets us into reverential notions of God again. Ideally, what I'd like to keep is huge respect for the fact that we were created by something or someone marvelous, who is not wholly unlike ourselves. Therefore, we can identify with that God, identify with God's drama as well as our own and thereby feel larger. Not, "Oh, God, oh, God, don't punish me, please!" Or, "God, dear God, please help me!" The reason I've never found Islam the least bit attractive is, you know, the prayer ritual. Kneel down, present your buttocks to the sky, and recognize that you are totally weak before the wrath of God. Well, we're totally weak before anything and everything that is vastly larger than ourselves. If this is what religion consists of—the recognition of being totally weak and that God will take care of us, provided we never cross any one of a thousand carefully laid-out lines of behavior—then I have to believe that existence is knotted up. And of course, the unspoken root of the nightmare in so much of Islam is precisely their present deep-seated fear. "What if we're wrong?" they have to be thinking. "We've been doing it this way for 1,500 years—and now, where are we?" It's like someone who's been married for fifty years saying, "Have I been with the wrong woman all this while?" Conceive of the hate people could have for a church or a marriage if they left it after that many years.

*Let me shift our subject. What are the reasons—as far as you can
surmise—that a soul is chosen for reincarnation? Does God or His
aides choose to extinguish some hideous souls, or must the souls ac-
quiesce, give up, and, in effect, commit eternal suicide, go out of existence?*

Let's start with that. I think certain people can lose the desire to keep their soul alive. They've suffered too much, one
way or another. The soul is weary.

Gary Gilmore might be one example.

His soul was not too weary. On the contrary, he didn't
want his soul to die. He was the exact opposite. He wanted
his body to die so his soul wouldn't be extinguished. He felt if
he didn't seek the death penalty but stayed in jail for his remaining twenty or thirty years, his soul would expire from
the sheer misery of living in jail, the emptiness of it, the ongoing, endless emptiness of living in prison if you'd already
used up, as he had, all its few vital possibilities. But there are
other people who might say, "Let my soul expire. It doesn't
deserve to go on"—which, by the way, is a thought that can
also come to the rottennest human alive, a part that says,
"You really are a swine; you don't deserve to live any longer.
You're much worse than you think you are." We all have
comparable sentiments (in lesser degree) when we arrive at a
reckoning with ourselves. But for some, it's terminal. They
are drenched in a mortal weariness of their own soul. So certain souls expire; they are ready to.

Generally speaking, however, most souls are probably not

willing to die that easily. On the other hand, the soul may not have the vigor to pass through endless reincarnations. If a cat has nine lives, what does a human soul possess? Three lives? It's boundlessly speculative, comically so. But then you are asking, How does God choose? How do God and His aides choose?

Can God execute a soul?

Why not? How not? God can create us, God can end us—which is part of the huge fear people have of God. God can terminate us. Absolutely.

But God hates to give up on an interesting artistic possibility in a human. So let's say He might take very bad people and have them reincarnated. Why? Is it to fill out the picture, to have a certain darkness, a few shadows for a certain corner? That is one of the clerical responses to explain why God tolerates evil. Of course, I would argue with that. I would say God sees wonderful potentialities in awful people. One of the reasons they *were* so awful was because they had large potentialities that became frustrated early and so turned into their opposites. Concerning this particular soul, therefore, God wants to try again. Or, to the contrary, take the case of someone who is perfectly bland and pleasant, good and decent, yet God is not vitally interested. That soul has done about what it's going to do and is no longer interesting to the Lord's higher purpose. God might then decide, We can only reincarnate him or her in an animal. We have to see if that soul responds to a more arduous life. Or God may decide—not worth repeating: Just as an artist can be ruthless, so can God when it comes to humans with mediocre lives. So reincarnation is, I think, the nexus of judgment.

For example, if someone has an adventurous soul, but physically they were weakened by early childhood illnesses, they might be endowed with more strength next time out. God could send them to stronger parents. But that could also produce larger demands. To justify God's new intention, you might have to become a skilled athlete. Think of what you'd have to endure to get there. Does this soul, interesting at present, have such capacity or not? God is experimenting. God is looking to find out. God, like a parent, learns from what the children accomplish and from where they fail. Why not assume that, with all else, we are also part of an enormous spiritual laboratory?

I'm still having trouble understanding how evolution and reincarnation—which are both part of your scheme—mesh. Did they begin simultaneously? Evolution, with its attempts to make species stronger, better, more durable, fits your scheme well. And reincarnation is often seen as an upward ladder, although souls can often go down as well as up. The idea of reincarnation, after all, is improvement, moral progress. Are both reincarnation and evolution completely controlled by God? Are their purposes intertwined?

I've been saying all along, God does not control our destiny.

No, I understand, but—

God can move in and control our destiny in special cases. But it may not be economic of His energy for a divinity to look to direct every one of us. God may just not be master of such resources. Rather, God learns from us. We learn from God, and God learns from us. This is a family relationship of the deepest sort. The parent can be enriched by the child; the child acquires strength and wit from the parent.

We can't think of God in terms of age, but we can certainly see ourselves in that manner. There are periods where we may get more from God—when we're young, for example. When we're old, we may be obliged to give back more, not necessarily to God but to the way we influence other people, the way we amplify His or Her vision or worsen it. Indeed, there are some things God can learn only from contemplating our direct experience. So God may be with us a good deal of the time. With certain people, I think God and the Devil are there most often. Certain kinds of highly dynamic people, certain kinds—just to take a flier on this—certain kinds of entertainers. They may be full of God and the Devil every moment they are onstage because there's such charisma in them and such lightning changeability. It's so difficult to know if you're dealing then with someone who's good, evil, or exceptional.

You still haven't told me how reincarnation interacts with evolution. What is their relation?

What would it be? We're talking about the macroeconomic and the microeconomic. Reincarnation is micro. My point is, that to the degree that careful attention is given to one particular reincarnation, finally, it's not perfect. There are times when God is better at it than at other times.

It may be that after the double blow of the Holocaust and the atom bomb, reincarnation was mucked up badly. There was just too much to do. One example would be the ugliness of cities that were flattened by the war. The way they were re-built may have been necessary, but it certainly was dreadful—by-the-numbers architecture. It may be that people are finally much less interesting today than they were one hundred and two hundred years ago, when they didn't have flush toilets but did live with interesting windows and doors.

Do we have anyone around today who's as wonderful and marvelous and godawful as Baudelaire? No. The modern equivalent would probably be Andy Warhol.

IV

On the Authority of the Senses

MICHAEL LENNON: *You've spoken of the authority of the senses many times, quoting St. Thomas Aquinas or quoting Hemingway. What exactly is this authority based on? What empowers it? If God is your answer, then to complicate the question, can't we say that evil in all cultures has almost always been associated with the flesh and the senses?*

NORMAN MAILER: My basic premise proposes that there's a different mixture of God and the Devil in every one of us. Some of that variety creates the shape of our character. You'll hear one person say about another, "He's a good guy, he's stand-up, but he sure can be a son of a bitch." In ourselves and others, we find this constant interplay of good and bad.

If we are going to talk about these matters, I think we

would do well to approach them with the confidence that humans have the right to explore anything and everything— at our spiritual peril, but we do have the right. It seems to me—how to put it?—I see no reason for a divinity to put everything into a Book and expect that to be our only guide. He gave us free will. Or She gave us free will. Once again, let's leave gender out of it. If we were given free will, then the Book is the first obstacle to it.

What's the role of the senses?

I would say the senses were given to us by God. If I'm ready to go in for speculations such as these, I would even go so far as to say that mind may have been the contribution of the Devil—or, at least, more so than God. How can I justify such a remark? Animals seem to function extraordinarily well on their instincts and their senses. To a large degree, they have community—ants, bees, all the way up to primates. There is an extraordinary amount of communication we can witness in animals, and they are undeniably superior to us in one manner: They don't go around slaughtering one another in huge numbers. If, by every other mode of moral judgment, we see ourselves as superior, still we know that animals left to themselves are not going to destroy the universe. But we could. So it may be a true question: Did the Devil invent mind? Or is this still God's domain? Or, more likely, does the search for dominance there become the field of battle?

There is no question in my mind that the Devil did enter mind. And, not being the first Creator, did His best to invade the senses as well, to corrupt the senses. But the question is sufficiently complex to assume that the senses are neither wholly God given nor Devil ridden.

But the line you quoted, which has puzzled me for decades, is "Trust the authority of the senses."

St. Thomas Aquinas said that, and Hemingway, in his way: "If it feels good, it is good." I've never read Aquinas in depth, but I was taken with the notion that the most formal of the Catholic philosophers had presented this rule of thumb. What I think it means—leave Aquinas out of it—is that we must trust the authority of the senses because that is the closest contact we have to the Creator; however, it is a most treacherous undertaking. As anyone who's ever enjoyed a drink knows, the authority of the senses on a boozy spree is exceptional. You feel so much, see so much—and that's even more true on marijuana. You trust the authority of the senses until, perhaps, they become so intense that God and the Devil seem to be there working with you full-time. We've all had the experience of an extraordinary trip on drink and/or pot, but what I know is that the end result is as often disaster as happiness. I won't pretend that every time you get drunk beyond measure nothing good will happen. It occurred to me at a certain point in my life that I had never, up to that moment, gone to bed with a woman for the first time without being drunk. Since some of the most important experiences of my life occurred that way, I can hardly wish to argue that drink serves the Devil alone. Given the rigors of modern society, it's possible we'd never get anywhere without liquor or pot.

You have me thinking of Blake's line: "The road of excess leads to the palace of wisdom."

It's implicit in what I just said, but I think I'd be happier if the line had gone: "The road of excess *can lead* to wisdom." I'm not in favor of excess because I've ruined too much in just that way. Blake did have an apocalyptic mind, which he served manfully, full-time. It's one of the reasons his remarks inspire the highest flights of fancy. But on the other hand, he is seen by our modern spirit as signally impractical.

The other thing you said that gave me pause was how the Devil invades mind. On more than one occasion you have suggested that scientific thinking undercuts metaphoric, intuitive thinking, and I wonder if that is what you see as the invasion of mind by the Devil. Scientific method, logic, linear thinking is opposed to the leaps of intuition in metaphor.

Often. It seems to me our minds work on two disparate systems. One is based on the senses. Metaphor, for example, is almost impossible without being somewhat attuned to nature, to its often subtle shifts of mood. That depends so much on one's senses. But then there is another faculty of mind that can be as cold as the polar cap. Indeed, it is a readiness to repel the senses, distrust them, even calumniate them as powers of distortion. This readiness to free oneself from the senses may be exercised most by the Devil.

Almost everything I dislike in the modern world is superrational: the corporation, the notion that we can improve upon nature, to tinker with it egregiously, dramatically, extravagantly. Nuclear bombs, as one example, came out of reason. It's not that scientists, filled with an acute sense of their own senses, brought their creative intimations to the atom bomb. On the contrary, it was an abstraction away from the senses, a pure flight of mind that came to the conclusion that it was possible to make the bomb—and then, that it had to be done, not only to defeat Japan but for the furtherance of science itself.

This may be related. I'd like to talk about Thomas's Gospel, where it's made clear that human beings have the obligation to bring forth what is within.

You had better say what this particular Gospel is.

Thomas's Gospel is, of course, not in the Bible but is a suppressed apocrypha, discussed most recently by Elaine Pagels. In her book, Thomas's Gospel states that as human beings, we all have the obligation to "bring forth what is within." And if we do, it will save us. If you keep in what is in, repress it, whatever it is—it will destroy you.

I used to believe that entirely. I now think it to be generally true but risky. Because what does it mean to bring forth what is within? I work on the notion that there's godliness within us and diabolism as well. So to bring forth what is within you, it is necessary, very often, to send out the worst elements of yourself. Because if they stay within, they can poison you. That is much more complex than saying, "Get it out! Act it out. Be free, man! Liberate yourself." Because very often what comes out is so bad that it injures others, sometimes dreadfully. You could say that every crime of violence is a way of getting the ugliness in oneself out, acting it out, doing it. You could even advance the argument that there are people who will contain what is ugly within them—and that's their honor. It's a complex matter—often there are people who will sacrifice themselves in order not to injure others. For example, if you act out something dreadful in yourself—if, for example, the need to get falling-in-the-gutter drunk thereby intensifies the miseries of everyone in your family—it is doing nothing good for others. Or excessive gambling. Or beating children. Or entering sexual relations with them. To the degree that certain ugly emotions are acted out, others are injured terribly by your freedom to do so. I could argue that it is often a Devil's urge you are expressing.

You have to ask yourself at a given moment, "Who is speaking within me?"

How do you answer that?

Well, I can give you one story; it's fascinated me for years. At a certain time in my life, I was feeling rocky. My third wife had decided she didn't want to go on with our marriage at a time when I had been hoping, "Maybe this time I can start to build a life." She was a very interesting woman but easily as difficult as myself. So when she broke it up, I didn't know where I was. And I remember one night, wandering around Brooklyn through some semi-slums—not the hard slums but some of the tougher neighborhoods a mile or two out from my house in Brooklyn—not even knowing what I was looking for, but going out, drinking in a bar, sizing up the bar, going to another bar, looking . . . this is ironic, but in those days, you actually would go to a bar and look for a woman. I think you still can, but it's been so long now since I did it that I can no longer speak with authority. Anyway, I found no woman. I went into an all-night diner—because I realized I was hungry, not only drunk but hungry—and ordered a doughnut and coffee, finished it. Then a voice spoke to me. I think it's one of the very few times I felt God was speaking to me. Now, of course, one can be dead wrong. I go back to Kierkegaard— just when you think you're being saintly, you're being evil; when you think you're being evil, you might be fulfilling or abetting God's will at that point. In any event, this voice spoke to me and said, "Leave without paying."

It was a minor sum—twenty-five cents for coffee and a doughnut in those days. I was aghast, because I'd been brought up properly. One thing you didn't do was steal. And never from strangers! How awful! I said, "I can't do it." And the voice—it was most amused—said, "Go ahead and do it," quietly, firmly, laughing at me. So I got up, slipped out of the restaurant, and didn't pay the quarter. And I thought about this endlessly. If it was God . . . as I said, this was the closest I ever came to trusting the authority of my senses. My senses told me this was a divine voice, not a diabolical one. It seemed to me that I was so locked into petty injunctions on how to behave, that on the one hand I wanted to be a wild man, yet I couldn't even steal a cup of coffee. To this day, I think it was God's amusement to say, "You little prig. Just walk out of there. Don't pay for the coffee. They'll survive, and this'll be good for you."

Now, I've thought about this often because it's a perfect

example of how difficult it is for us to know at a given moment whether we're near to God or to Satan, which is why Fundamentalists can drive you up the wall—their sense of certainty is the most misleading element in their lives. It demands, intellectually speaking, spiritually speaking, that one must remain at a fixed level of mediocrity. It's a great irony, because many of them who are good Christians, or Orthodox Jews, are compassionate. I don't know much about Islam, but I'm sure the same is true there. You can have fine people, wonderful people, Fundamentalists full of compassion . . . can say in passing, If God was ever going to mingle in our affairs, Christ is more than a metaphor. Compassion is probably the finest emotion we humans can have. When tears come to our eyes for the sorrow of someone else, that may be as close as we get to reaching the best element in ourselves. But, there again, it's difficult to know how pure any moment of compassion is. And any false variety of it can be toxic. When it is manufactured by constant adjurations applied to the daily habits of Fundamentalists, compassion can become the opposite of itself, and turn into an instrument for power. "Follow me because I feel compassion for you."

Speaking crudely, if half the Fundamentalists in the world are truly compassionate, the other half are on an egregious power-trip.

You know, this always stops me. I try to think how you would translate your metaphysics, your cosmology, into an ethical system. It's not just the Fundamentalists. Most religious systems say: "OK, we have the theology, now let us show you how that translates into ethics." But what you tell me over and over again is, "We can't be sure." It would be very difficult to construct an ethical system by which to live one's life based on your scheme of beliefs. Have you thought of that?

I accept your point. I do search for an ethic I can believe in. And that is where I go back to trusting the authority of my senses. They can also be—what's the word I'm looking for?—traduced. To the degree that the Devil may affect our senses, they can become a perfect place for Him to get to us. That would be the Devil's aim exactly—to enter our senses, make us feel we are having a godly emotion, when in fact we are being inspired by the Devil.

So I hope I never construct an ethic by offering a few bones. The worst to be said about Fundamentalism is that it reduces people to the reflexes of a good dog. If a good dog is upset, give it a treat.

Fundamentalism is comfortable.

It's comfortable, but it is limiting. I keep going back to Kierkegaard, who, for my money, was probably the most profound Christian. He searched into the complexity of our relation not only to divinity but to diabolism as well. He knew that we must take nothing for granted in the moral firmament. We cannot kneel forever before the neon sign that purports to be God's mystery: "Don't ask, just obey!"

We can, of course, for the sake of this argument, pay another visit to the subject of Fundamentalism. After all, a good many Fundamentalists do function with vigor. Their lives have been simplified. They don't worry over questions that are debilitating. They function very well—at their medium level. No great writer ever came out of Fundamentalism, nor any great scientist. To my knowledge, very few talented actors came out of Fundamentalism—or stayed with it for long. Never a genius of any kind, not since Augustine and Aquinas.

So perhaps Fundamentalism is for the less daring, the less bold, the less gifted? But aren't you living on an ethical razor's edge, listening to inner voices to find the right word? That's not something everyone can emulate.

Yes, people want to live in such a way that they will feel secure. But there may be no such security available. Right now, parenthetically, we are living in a time where we have to wonder if we will even see the end of the twenty-first century. Or will we destroy ourselves? In that sense, directly, there is no spiritual security.

So the Fundamentalists, beneath everything else, feel the same fears that existential thinkers suffer—that the whole thing can come to an end. Fundamentalists look to alleviate that fear by way of what I would call their desperate belief that it's "God's will" and at the end they will be transported to Heaven. Well, once again, this supposes that God is All-Good and All-Powerful and will carry the righteous right up there. Of course, that offers nothing to the idiocies of human history, particularly that the more we develop as humans, the worse we are able to treat one another. Why? Because we now have the power to destroy one another at higher, more unfeeling levels. This can be epitomized again and again by repeating the familiar example I take from the concentration camps—telling poor wretches that they're going to have a shower to get rid of lice, and instead they die with a curse in their hearts. That's more hideous, in a certain sense, than dropping a bomb on one hundred thousand people—on people you know nothing about. And yet you have Fundamentalists carrying on about abortion, speaking of it as thwarting God's will. What does it have to do with God's will if you kill a thousand people in one minute with gas? Or destroy hundreds of thousands in an instant of atomic man-made lightning from the sky? What does that do to God's will?

We might assume that God, like us, is doing the best that can be done under the circumstances. God is our Creator. God put us here. We are God's artistic vision, we are God's children, if you will, and it's not a good parent who looks always to control the child. The mark of a good parent is that he or she can take joy in the moment when a developing child begins to outstrip the parent. God is immensely powerful but is *not* All-Powerful. God is powerful enough to give us lightning and thunder and extraordinary sunsets, incredible moments where we appreciate God's sense of beauty. But if God is All-Powerful, then how can you begin to explain the monstrosities of modern history? There are theological arguments by great theologians that these horrors are to test us. But this reduces our concept of God to a stage director who says, "Let the actors follow the script. Do not give them access to the playwright."

In one of our earlier conversations, you said humans were created by someone or something not unlike ourselves. So we are then, in some way, created in the image of God?

Yes. I believe that.

Doesn't that suggest we are more good than evil?

Potentially more good. When a good man and a good woman have a child, there's every reason to believe that child will be a good person. But it's not guaranteed. Good parents can have evil children.

If we're created in God's image and we're potentially good but then choose evil, perhaps we were evil all along.

Look at your phrase—"evil all along." If, at Creation, the Devil was present and entered us as well, then what we speak of as original sin can be seen as God's obligatory collaboration with the Devil. We were born good and evil.

Fifty-fifty?

The point is, whether it's fifty-fifty, sixty-forty, seventy-thirty, the odds change in each of us because there's an intense war that goes on forever, not only between God and the Devil but—I've said this before—God and the Devil as they war within us. We make our own bargains with Them. God and the Devil do not have the resources to be in complete control of us all the time. It isn't as if we walk through a normal day, and there's God on one shoulder and the Devil on the other—not at all. They come to us when we attract their attention, because it affects Their interest as well as ours.

What I use as the notion behind these assumptions that divine energy is analogous to human energy—it is not inexhaustible. God and the Devil are each obliged to manage their own economies of energy, which is to say that they will give more attention to certain elements of human behavior than to others. Very often, they withdraw from certain people. Too much is being given, too little is coming back.

Given this supposition, I feel more ready to make an approach to the question of ethics. It must be obvious in all I've said so far that I not only am an existentialist but would go so far as to say that we do not know our nature. We only find out about ourselves as we proceed through life. And as we do, we open more questions.

Jean Malaquais once made a splendid remark—at least for me—during the course of a lecture. He was a brilliant lecturer, and in the middle of a verbal flight—this was at the New School—some kid said bitterly, "You never give us answers. You only pose questions." And Jean stopped in the full flight of his rhetoric and replied, "There are no answers. There are only questions."

The point is that the purpose of life may be to find higher and better questions. Why? Because what I believe—this is wholly speculative but important to me—is that we are here as God's work, here to influence His future as well as ours. We are God's expression, and not all artworks are successful. But we are here because God has a vision of existence that is at odds with other visions of existence in the universe. There we get into the real question of cosmic hegemonies. There may be a majordomo at the core, maybe not. There may be gods—the heavens may be analogous to pagan times. These gods are fighting for dominance over one another.

So we come back once more to "Where is the ethic?" And again I return to trusting the authority of our senses. What now do I mean by that? Isn't it true that as we free ourselves of false conceptions of what life might be, as we free ourselves of the maxims and injunctions other people have put into us from childhood, as we come to have a better sense of "whatever I am, I am beginning to have my own ideas," you can also develop some instinct that one is doing the right thing or one is not. Or, all too often, one is not doing much. As we get older, "Not much at all" can take over most of our lives. If I am doing a crossword puzzle, there is no high motive necessarily involved. Instead, the activity might be to some most modest degree on the side of evil—I'm consuming time that could be spent in better ways. Or, to the contrary, I might be preparing my system to get ready for something worthwhile. It's not a large question: I do the crossword puzzle, and I don't think about it as good or evil. And I don't think of myself as good or evil so much as probably leaning slightly in the right direction or the wrong one when it comes down to how I am exercising my time.

So if you ask where the ethic is at any moment, it can be no more than that one is the resultant of all the forces that are in you as that vector confronts all the forces supporting you and opposing you. It's as if we live in a triangular relationship with God and the Devil, trying to sense the best thing to do at a given moment, be it a good thing or a bad thing. Let me go back to what might have been my lone visitation from the

Lord. What God might have been trying to tell me was, "Get over this notion of good, right, proper. Because very often when you're moving in a direction you think improper, you might be helping Me more than when you're trying to be proper. Because when you're trying to be proper, you could be poisoning yourself with frustrated annoyance that makes you a colder person and of less use to Me."

What I'm offering to people as an ethic is to have the honor to live with confusion. Live in the depths of confusion with the knowledge back of that, the certainty back of that—or the belief, the hope, the faith, whatever you wish to call it—that there is a purpose to it all, that it is not absurd, that we are all engaged in a vast cosmic war and God needs us. That doesn't mean we can help God by establishing a set of principles to live by. We can't. Why not? Because the principles vary. The cruelest obstacle to creating one's own ethic is that no principle is incorruptible. Indeed, to cleave to a principle is to corrupt oneself. To shift from one principle to another can, however, be promiscuous. Life is not simple. Ethics are almost incomprehensible, but they exist. There is a substratum of moderate, quiet, good feeling. Generally, if I'm doing things in such a way that the sum of all my actions at the moment seems to be feasible and responsible and decent, that certainly gives me a better feeling than if I am uneasy, dissatisfied with myself, and not liking myself.

Now, obviously, there is room for error. We all know about vanity. There are people who, when they like themselves, are dangerous. When they think they are extraordinary and fabulous, they can be awful.

*So it isn't so much that you have no ethical system but one that can-
not be abstracted nor carved on tablets for people to carry around
and consult whenever they have to make a decision. Life is always
more complicated than any rule that can be laid down.*

What I'm asking for. . . . This is an odd analogy, but not
entirely. There are certain people who worship sex, good sex.
I might be one of them. What I've noticed about good sex,
when it's really good, is the extreme sensitivity with which
you proceed. At a given moment, it's a creative dance. There
is such a thing as a pure act of love when every moment is dis-
tinctive and lovely and fine. That does happen. For most people, it happens so rarely that they remember it—and then
remember it and remember it. A sense of perfection does live
in our concept of sex.

In the same way, sometimes, for short periods in our lives,
I think there's an analogous sense of perfection to all sorts of
basic emotions—in love, in nurture, in caring for people, in
grieving, in mourning. It's very hard to mourn, mourn openly
and honestly. Mourning is an element in people's lives that
can be duplicitous, even ugly. Take a wife who's been married
to a man for forty years—and in her mourning, what if she
detects a secret spot of glee? "That selfish bastard is finally
gone." So mourning can be shocking for people because they
discover sides of themselves they never knew existed—or the
reverse. Sometimes people die whom you thought you didn't
care that much about, and you discover you have lost something or someone valuable to you. So there is the constant element of discovering yourself—not in the time-consuming
way people do in psychoanalysis, where every little act has to

be analyzed and reanalyzed until the air in the room is stale.
Rather, just like making love, it's a matter of being sensitive to
the moment, reflecting the moment as best you can. And that
is not an easy matter. You want a few general ethical principles from me? Remarks I'd even offer to a stranger? Well,
then, if possible, I would say to the stranger, "Give up smok-
ing." Because that tends to block a good deal of sensitivity in
yourself. It serves the will. I used to smoke two packs a day—
why? Because it served my will, particularly when it came to
writing. Took me a year to learn how to begin writing again
once I did give it up. Perhaps I became a better writer. My
point is, anything that will enable you to get closer to yourself, good or bad . . . in other words, being close to oneself
can be much more unpleasant than being at a distance from
oneself. That is why most people do choose, indeed, to be a
bit removed from themselves. And so often—here's the dirty
little secret—that's why they smoke.

*But you know, I remember something else you said about getting
close to yourself. It's stuck with me. I don't even remember where
you said it—you might have brought it up in conversation—but
you declared: "If you dig deep enough into yourself, you're going to
come out your asshole."*

[N.M. laughs]

*In other words, yes, there are doors, and you must open many of
those doors, and the ensuing doors within doors, but every once in a
while you want to be careful about what you open.*

Well, of course, you have to be careful about certain doors.
Anyone who flings everything ajar at once would be blown

away. A mighty change could rage through all the rooms in your psyche. One of the most jealously self-protective elements in human nature may be to protect oneself from one's own dark and barricaded corners.

So I don't think it's a real problem that we're going to open, by mistake, *all* the doors at once—we don't. We can't. What I meant by the closer you get to yourself, the closer you are to coming out of your own asshole has to do with something I'd like to attach to this discussion concerning the nature of defecation, shit, and waste. It may be worth getting into. As a small premise, think of people who are terribly prudish about evacuation. They don't want to think about it, don't talk about it, it's beneath them, they hope it is terribly far away from them. I'd say, ethically speaking, that's not a comfortable way to be. Far better that when you're sitting on the throne—parenthetically, it's interesting that we have that metaphor, "the throne," precisely for the toilet—when you're sitting on the throne, you do well to be regal about it and enjoy the sniffs of your own waste. Smell your own shit and decide for yourself if you're a little more healthy or a little more unhealthy than you thought you were the last time you sat down. That's part of being close to yourself. You take this notion that what comes out of you may be unpleasant, but it is certainly real. It can be the nearest we come to a fact. It's like hearing your own voice unexpectedly—so often it's too shrill, too arrogant, too peremptory, too spoiled, or harsh. To the degree we can hear our own voice, we improve our relations with other people. Because if we find our own voice unpleasant at times, then if the other person starts shrieking at us, we don't have to think, "How unstable is the other." Not if we can recognize that our own voice was ugly enough to incite the response.

That's one of the elements in a decent marriage.

This being attuned and listening and paying attention to the self . . . as you were speaking, I kept thinking, "This is positively Jamesian." James would sense the tiniest shifts in perception. Now, he probably wasn't interested in smelling shit very much—not at all.

That may have been his one major deficiency. *[Laughter]*

A while ago, you were hammering on Revelation as something to be rejected by human experience. In your view, is there any merit or value in the holy books of the great religions, or do you think they should be seen as historical artifacts, quaint, useless curiosities?

No, no.

What is their use then?

Well, if they're seen as general principles rather than as absolute dicta, they can be of great use. The Ten Commandments—most of us do react within the framework of those ten injunctions. The point is not to build up an inner sense of self-righteousness—"I obey the Ten Commandments, and therefore I am nearer to God." No, they are crude guides. "Do not kill." Well, yes, do not kill. Does that mean you have to piss in your pants if you have a gun in your hand and you're face-to-face with Adolf Hitler in 1941? No, you kill him. At that point, I would not consider "Do not kill" an absolute command.

Let's go through the Ten Commandments: Most of them are so simple they apply to 90 percent of the cases. But you have some . . . Do not commit adultery." Well, there it can become more complex. Because when people are engaged in miserable marriages, their lives are foul; their children's lives are poisoned. And at a given moment, there's an impulse to escape, to commit adultery in order to avoid doing worse things, like screaming too much at the kids.

Where the Ten Commandments fall down is that there are times you have to do something deemed worse than what you're supposed to do. Because if you don't do that something worse, you're going to get into actions even more destructive, more evil, more unhappy, more toxic to others.

So you're not interested in jettisoning the great holy books of the world; you just want to qualify them.

Not qualify. I want us to cease looking upon them slavishly. Once one becomes a peon to any part of one's mind, one is then open to the dark side of the moon, which is mass destruction.

Your position is very much like Emerson's. He revered Jesus, he was interested in all the holy books, but he certainly wasn't going to be bound by them. His own quest for his inner self, very much like yours, precluded that.

I've read Emerson but only in passing, and that for a simple reason. One, I think he's a great writer, and two, I did feel close enough to him to think, "If I study him, I could end up trying to write wonderful pieces about Emerson." My arrogance, my vanity, if you will, is that I am out on my own explorations. I've had that rare experience, probably analogous to Emerson's, of being successful enough at an early age not to worry about making a living the way other people do. In return for that blessing, the least I could do was spend my time thinking. I have had such an advantage, and it's an enormous one, and I'm aware of it. I'm happy I'm aware of it because it keeps me modest rather than vain. There were years when I was much too vain, and I have paid for that. Vanity is corrosive.

There are a few generalities you can count on—vanity is immensely dangerous. But nothing is absolute. Vanity may be terribly important for people who don't have enough of it, even as it's injurious to people who have too much. But then the notion of moderation that comes to us from the Greeks can also be stultifying. If you apply it to dangerous activities, however, it becomes interesting. What is moderation for a top-notch race-car driver? What's moderation to a libertine? Well, you don't have to pursue every last fuck that's open to you. What's the mark of moderation in a womanizer, a groper? He doesn't have to feel every woman's ass he's inclined to explore. He looks to be discriminating. When action is high, the road back to balance is discrimination.

A phrase comes to mind—I'm sure you won't like it—that, crudely speaking, applies to a lot of what you've been saying, and that's "situation ethics."

You mean: "Do the right thing." It's a maxim often used by black kids. First, what does "do the right thing" mean? The kids are talking then about situations fewer whites have considered in their full complexity. You're a drug dealer, and you're cutting your stuff, and there's a customer who, on the one hand, is a fool—you can take him completely and give him something close to plain talcum powder. On the other hand, you can see he really needs a drug at that moment. So "do the right thing"—don't cut his stuff to a ridiculous level. Lose a little of the profit.

At every level of human existence, no matter how evil certain activities may seem to others, there is a caution present along with the ugly impulse (except, of course, for those rare occasions when the unholy impulse takes over entirely). But short of such moments, I would say that even very unpleasant people will hold back on certain occasions because we all do have this sense of "do the right thing."

My basic argument is that ethics is not a system of rules—as you said, not something you can etch in stone. Ethics is a sensitivity to the moment and the thought: "This is probably better to do than that." It could even come down to calculation: You're bilking someone in a deal. But if you're going to bilk him, better not to do it in too ugly a manner, or you'll increase his desire to take advantage of others. So what's your ethos at that moment? It's to reduce ugliness in the world system—by a little.

In one of our earlier conversations, you spoke of a time in the distant future when, after some "definitive metamorphosis of existence," human vision would join God's vision—perhaps—and travel across the heavens.

When did I say that?

In one of our earlier conversations.

Was that toward the end of *Ancient Evenings* or in *Of a Fire on the Moon?*

Elements of that were there. You were looking around the corner, so to speak; you were anticipating, rare for you, how things might possibly turn out. A "definitive metamorphosis of existence" was part of the phrase, as I recall. Human nature would shift into a completely different level; human vision would become married with God's and, I assume, would then split off from the demonic. At that point, something would happen—we would "travel across the heavens."

Well, that's apocalyptic. I do not see any way we're going to separate drastically or quickly from the Devil as well as from God.

So you would not see—

At present, I am more concerned that we do not destroy ourselves.

What would be the necessary conditions for this metamorphosis of existence to happen? What would human beings have to become?

Some of it may be obvious: more and then even more self-awareness. More freedom from Fundamentalism. More readiness for humans to accept the heroic demand that they stop leaning on God, stop relying on God, and start realizing that God's needs could be greater than ours, God's woes more profound than our own. God's sense of failure may be so deep as to mock our sense of failure. God, I believe, is, at present, far from fulfilling His own vision. He is mired in our corporate promotions all over the globe, our superhighways, our plastic, our threats of nuclear warfare, our heartless, arrogant, ethnic wars, our terrorism, our spread of pollution all over His environment. How can God's sorrow not be immeasurably greater than ours?

Before we can approach any thoughts of apocalypse, we have to become human enough, brave enough, to recognize that we cannot rely on God. Rely too much on God, and we are comparable to a tremendously selfish child who drives a parent into exhaustion, deadens the parent through endless demands. "Save me! God, please, can I have that beautiful dress I want for the high school prom? Thank you, God, deliver it to me, God." *[Pause]* "If you don't, God, I'll be angry at you," is the underlying element in so many of the prayers. Or the abject beseechment—"God, have pity on me, I'm a poor worm."

I think we become a hint more heroic if we recognize that we do have to stand on our own. So I can feel a certain respect for atheists. I have huge disagreements with them—the first might be the absolute refusal of a majority to consider the notion of karma for even a moment. Or any kind of Hereafter—their determined intensity that there will be nothing after life. This creates its own sort of trouble. It fortifies the liberal notions that we have to take care of people we know nothing about and enter strange countries and provide them with democracy, whether they desire it or not. Needless to say, Christians have been doing the same for a long time.

I have a tremendous distrust of what people think is the good. At any given moment, 90 percent of that is fashion. The war in Iraq is a perfect example of fashion—the bright idea that we are there to inject democracy into any country that needs it. That was a political fashion; it had no real basis in political reality. Of course, it can be done, you can always inject some warped form of democracy into a country if you have enough troops and are ready to ignore the cost.

I want to come back one more time to love and courage. Here I'm going to use Henry James—his idea of the greatest human act, one that required both love and courage, is an act of renunciation. At the heart of all his novels is an act of renunciation, and usually it's a quiet act, not even an act you take credit for.

It's suspicious in James, because James's life is a study in renunciation. I distrust authors, especially very good authors, when they lay out a full program for their characters that is covertly supporting their own work. James had too little passion to get near to people he didn't understand. He worked out an immensely elaborate and beautiful art, but it's full of renunciation. And we pay the price. If he had been greater as a writer, Americans would be that much better off. James is not much of a guide to the modern world. He's a marvelous guide when you're younger to understanding some of the subtly disproportionate things that go on in high society. He's a great guide to a very limited mountain pass that few people will ever have to traverse. But renunciation did him in. If James had had a few passionate love affairs and had been able to write about them—

He saw them as antithetical. It's the life/art division. James be-
lieved that you can have a life or you can have the art, and I'm
going to have the art.

Look, I agree, and that does not surprise me, particularly
now that I'm old. Recently, I've been saying that if you want
to be a serious novelist, a large element of it is monastic. It's a
dull life in the daily sense.

That's very Jamesian.

You don't have a lot of fun. You have to give up the idea of
fun.

Renunciation serves art. That was his dictum.

In that sense, I do agree. But there is renunciation as a
working sacrifice, a temporary renunciation, and there's vis-
ceral renunciation, which can amputate a novelist's taproot.

He should have broken off the reservation once in a while? Gone off
on a toot?

Yes. Once you've had a wild time or two, you can often
support your imagination for a long time. In the harshest
sense, you can say the trouble with Henry James is he never
fucked another human.

I have one last question, which I think you've already answered.
Your position on Jesus seems to be very similar to the position of the
Muslims: They revere him as a teacher, a prophet, a guide—they do
not recognize him as anything special beyond one in a long line—

No. I wouldn't say I have that point of view. It's possible, to me, that Jesus is the Son of God. If God wants to inspire humankind, which is after all His Creation, why couldn't He, why wouldn't He, send a part of Himself to humankind? I can accept the miracle—miracles don't bother me. What irks me is the bric-a-brac put up to surround the miracle.

So the incarnation—the Word made Flesh is something—

The Word made Flesh gives me trouble. The Gospel of John makes me uneasy. I think John, more than Matthew, Mark, or Luke, created some of the unhappier aspects of the Church. The notion of the Word made Flesh can be reversed—there's the danger. The Flesh can be turned into the Word, can become injunctions, direct communication, usually from above straight down. What is totalitarianism but the Word being implanted in the Flesh?

But John said you have to believe Revelation, it's all there, there's no other way. Whereas Thomas said you have to look inside yourself, John said, "Forget what's inside yourself, look to the Gospels." So you'd have a natural animosity to John.

I do—and the Flesh was transmogrified into the Word. Most of us by now live with the Word, not the Flesh.

But don't you find the Gospel of John superior in its writing?

The writing is better, yes, which is why people love John and why, of the four, he's the most important. But he is tethered to the word that he helped to create—those loud-voiced, lying, Bible-thumping exhortation disseminators on TV who are also ready to sweep up your dollars, dear fellow Jesus lovers, fellow servants to the Word and the Book, just send it to me here at blank-blank dot com.

V

Saints

MICHAEL LENNON: *I would like to take up again the question of saints. I think you need to say more. In most religions, saints do play a tremendous role. They intercede for lesser humans. They give witness to God's greatness. They are models for humanity by their ability to withstand suffering. Indeed, some of their suffering is self-imposed. Do you see saints in the same way as in the traditional religions?*

NORMAN MAILER: You reach me on a weak point. I don't know that I have a good deal to say. It does make sense to me that there are certain people whom God would feel close to. I suppose the subtext to such a remark is that God may not feel equally near to each one of us. In truth, I would doubt that He does. After all, the Devil is always doing His best to obfuscate the divine venture. So it's not easy to reach us. Very few of us ever get a message directly from God or the Devil. (Of course, hysterics receive several a day.) Most of us are obliged to live with a subtle smudge upon our senses. Spiritually speaking, we inhabit a complex and contradictory environment. Theologically speaking, spiritually speaking, we may not be as near to ultimates as perhaps we were centuries ago.

Now there are people who succeed, one way or another, of divesting themselves of most of the Devil. It's hard for me to believe, however, that a saint can exist with nothing of the Satanic still residing in him or her. I can assume that saints are *relatively* pure, but the notion that they are absolutely so— well, given my temperament, it begs too many questions. It makes everything too easy. Because if saints are perfect, why the Hell do they fail so often? Does the Devil overtake them? Or—let me advance an essentially medieval argument—is the saint so good that the Devil has to use extraordinary and exhausting efforts to create a defeat, and so the saint serves God's purpose by wearing the Devil out?

But not all saints are defeated.

Give me an example of some triumphant saints.

St. Peter.

St. Peter! He deserted Christ three times.

But then he redeemed himself and started Christianity.

Yes, and Christianity may still be laboring under the fact that it was Peter who commenced it. You've got a three-time treacherous associate there—

There are other saints. . . .

I won't say that people can't repent, that they can't restore their spirits back to something finer, but nonetheless renegades do have to remain under suspicion.

That, in a way, brings me to my next question. Your God and your Devil are limited, and I assume—

Not limited but finite. Certainly not infinite.

I assume that human perfection is truly impossible for you, as you just said. If there were a human being who was All-Good, she or he would be better than God. And if we found an absolutely perfect human being, your theology would be hard-pressed to account for that person.

I don't think I'm in any danger of having my theology, such as it is, overthrown by that premise. Of course, there will never be a perfect human being. It's not in the range of our thinking. After all, I am going so far as to say there's no such thing as a perfect divinity. The nature of the universe is provisional, existential, not finally determined. That is at the core of everything I present here. God's future is as open as our own.

Let me return to saints. I can admit that St. Peter was not perfect. But think of St. Francis of Assisi. . . .

Yes, he's perfect in a beautiful way that took care of a great many animals, and thereby brought us a little more into sympathy with creatures who often feel more life than ourselves, but I don't know that he improved human nature particularly, not even by his fine example. I'm asking, rather, about the kind of saints who are trying to change human nature and almost always end up as martyrs. Indeed, the way they become saints is that they were martyrs first.

One way that we know a saint is a saint, at least in Christianity, is that he or she was martyred. St. Stephen was martyred. St. Perpetua was martyred.

But you mentioned animals. To shift for a moment: How far down does the chain of Being—or, if you will, the war between God and the Devil—manifest itself?

I have no idea.

You said that dogs have souls.

Yes.

Then I assume both sides have enlisted them. What about the other animals? Are you ready to say that some are on God's side? Are the eagles and the doves? The vultures and the snakes?

To enter these matters is equal to philosophical free-fall. I would rather rely on the sort of instinctive verdicts that humans come up with after centuries of dealing with certain problems. For instance, my belief in God and the Devil comes, to a good extent, from the fact that the majority of people, through all of recorded time, have believed in both evil spirits and good ones and, finally, in a god and a devil accompanied by angels and demons. If the majority have such beliefs, one does well to keep some respect for such notions.

Error is our human signature, but not a constant incapacity to perceive anything beyond ourselves.

Do you relate any of your ideas to modern concepts of disease?

Well, I hardly subscribe to the modern notion that all disease is evil and is to be eradicated at all cost, so that we can all live for centuries and populate the globe with ten trillion people. Life and death, I will repeat, do have an intimate relation to each other. Just as we cannot conceive of an existence where there is only daylight and never night, so I don't care to think of life void of death and rebirth. Since I believe that some of us do come back again, I will say that I haven't the remotest clue whom we may become in our next existences. It's possible, it's perfectly possible, that some or all of us have to descend to the bacteriological level and return from there. My guess, however, is that it is not so elaborate a chain of reincarnation. That would propose a most complex universe in the afterlife. I would rather assume there's a purpose to everything, including the biological agents that infect us and often kill us. It may be there are agents of death with which God experiments as fully as God experiments with the development of human and animal life.

You've talked a lot about the moment of death and the state of mind one is in at the moment of death—this follows, I think, from what you just said. Peace of mind, I think, is important to many religions—peace of mind at death—none more so than Catholicism. The Church actually has a sacrament called Extreme Unction, now called "Anointing of the Sick." It was created by the Church to give hope to people who were near death.

How would you say that the Church arrived at such confidence in its power?

Well, over millennia, the Church created seven sacraments. And the last one is Extreme Unction. I can't tell you which Father of the Church came up with the theology of it, but there is a sense of the Church reaching out to the individual at the moment of death and applying all of its powers to giving that person peace of mind as they pass over.

Or, at least, giving them a belief in peace of mind. . . .

From the Church's point of view, Extreme Unction works. I've seen people receive it—and you know, it does give them tremendous peace of mind.

I can believe it's effective. Certainly for devout Catholics, it would be. Let me tell you a small story about a dear friend of mine, Eddie Bonetti, who was dying of cancer. I spoke to him a day before he went. He was a marvelous fellow, and you'll see from the conversation what his positive qualities were.

We were talking on the phone, and he knew death was close. At a given moment, I said to him, "Eddie, are you scared?"

He said, "Yeah, Norman, I am."

I said, "Eddie, it seems to me you have less reason to be afraid than anyone I know. Because you're the loyalest guy I've ever met. You never turned your back on a friend, no matter how much it cost you. I really can't believe that something bad is waiting for you."

He said, "You really believe that, Norman?"

I said, "I think so, I really do."

And the woman he was living with at the time told me he did die later that day with a smile, which gave me heart because I loved the guy and so am tempted, naturally, to hope that my words had a little to do with his peace.

So, yes, I can believe that Extreme Unction can be wonderful for some. I will say I expect it's a human creation rather than a divine fact. There were no miracles announcing it, no revelation from God. This was a human attempt, if you will, to understand how God's mind works. So all right, yes, I can believe Extreme Unction is there for a devout Catholic. It might not work for someone like myself. If someone came in and said, "You are going to die in peace," I'd probably say, "Let me go. If you don't mind, I'll fine-tune my own end—you don't need to do it for me."

Certain theologians would say, "Well, this is vanity. This is precisely why you're not going to have a good end." And my feeling is, "Hey, pal, it's open. None of us knows. It doesn't matter how much tradition is behind it. Tradition *suggests* there may well be something powerful behind it, but can it fit every human case?"

Why is the state of mind at death so very important to you?

Because I think it's our point of departure, our angle of flight, if you will.

So what? Everybody has a bad day. You could happen to have a bad day on the day you die.

No, no—whenever you have a bad day, there's a lot of reason for the downer. I can give you twenty causes for such an hour. Some are serious, some are passing. But, no, I won't let you hide behind the notion that a bad day is no more than a slot on the roulette wheel.

But there are also days when we have false euphoria. We can feel good for no accountable reason and then the next day say, "Why did I feel so good? I still have all these problems!"

Whenever we have an emotion we can't account for, good or bad, I expect that the root is karmic. That may be the only visitation we receive from previous lives. By the laws of the game, which may well be basic and necessary, we can't know who we were and where we were in previous lives. Nonetheless, intense and unaccountable emotions can come from one's karmic past.

But I'm not answering your question. I think at the moment we die, we are the sum of all the good and bad we've done, all the courage and cowardice we've exercised. And so, for example, if we die with a desire to be reborn, I think it means a great deal to God. If you will, it's like reaching into a litter to select a pup, and there's one who catches our eye because he wants us. He is the one we choose to take home. Using that crude analogy, I would say that it's important to be ready. After all, that is the one situation we can't simulate, can't preempt. We can pretend to a huge number of emotions in our lives; we may well spend three quarters of our lives being what we are not. I would go so far as to say that one of the reasons people get married is so that they can stop acting for a period every day, an hour when they don't have to present a face to the world. People who live alone are always obliged to put on that other face when they leave their room.

So I would say that when one is close to death, at least if one knows one's going to die, there can be a desire for another life or a yearning toward peace or—and this is the worst condition—a wish to pass away altogether. The largest urge of the soul becomes "I don't want to feel pain, so I will accept nothingness."

And really, suppose you're on high, wondering which humans you'll refashion. Suppose there's a man that God is most interested in, but at the last moment that agent is pleading for stupor. God says, "Do I really want to go through this again? Have this person become one more large disappointment?"

To repeat: I do believe our final judgment in this life is given by the form of our rebirth. The only divine judgment we receive is our placement in the next life. If you have no desire to live again, God's decision may be, "No. No need to be reborn." True death. End of existence.

I want to explore this more. A nurse told me this recently, a hospice nurse who cared for the dying—three times a week she went through this, and she had great experience. She told me that at the end, often, because people were taking drugs, they'd be on morphine to cut the pain, and their personality, as she put it, "dissolves." They were alive, they were functioning, but their souls were already gone.

And so, for them, the death was before they died—the body was still breathing, the automatic systems were working, but . . . but indeed, the people I have seen die, they revert to powerful impulses, powerful atavistic impulses: the desire to keep oneself clean—they get on the toilet when they're dying. The desire to remember one's mother or grandmother. Or when someone touches you, the desire to reach out or, to the reverse, the fear you're going to be violated when you're lying on your bed. And I've seen that, the few deaths I've witnessed.

So people don't ordinarily die in moments of clarity, like Eddie Bonetti. Often they don't even know who they are.

I can't answer that. You can die spiritually an hour, a day, a month, or five years before your death. I think the more your soul can remain intact up to the extinction of your body, the finer candidate you are for reincarnation. But that's just my notion.

So risky. . . . You mean someone who really wants to be reborn but goes into a coma loses his or her shot?

Look, the soul can fight the body right down to the very end. The soul can say, "All right, I don't feel anything in my legs anymore. Nothing in my fingers. I can't find my thoughts, but I know what I want. That way is more life. I want to be reborn." Or, to the contrary, the soul can feel it isn't worth it. "Let the body have its day. I've abused this body all my life, it's now demanding a cruel payment and—let me tell the truth to myself—I'm bankrupt."

But I do think that the soul—taking this intelligence from your lady at the hospice—if it leaves a week or two before the body, I think, speaking in terms of the transmigration of souls, it could make for a few complexities. So many talk about death as a vision: There's this wonderful white light, and long-expired relatives come out to meet you. I'm a touch dubious about that. For some people, yes—they were close to their relatives, and their kin do come forth.

But there's an awful lot of spirit travel involved. Think of the logistics of such a Hereafter. God's energies, as I see them, are immense but, to repeat, not infinite. So there are all sorts of procedures to be followed after you die. Economic procedures, if you will, involving the energies available to the Hereafter. It may be much more complex and less adaptable than we assume. The more flaming, fiery, flamboyant sects, the ones who promise everything in the Hereafter, bring out my cynicism (which, after all, is my shield against wishful thinking). Often, I expect, in the immediate hours or days after our deaths there can be pauses, long waits in a vast hall—somewhat like the first day in the army, when nobody knew what to do with you, and you were not yet assigned to some sort of temporary training platoon. We can talk about Limbo a little later if you wish. Limbo may be an absolutely realistic station for most people when they die. They hang around for quite a while.

Limbo can be for years.

Well, I don't know. I think it could also be a matter of divine bureaucratic—dare I say it?—mismanagement. Because bureaucratic mismanagement on earth—I don't know that we necessarily have to assume all this changes in the Hereafter. I don't think angels are perfect any more than I believe demons are totally evil. I think the rarest condition in existence is absolute purity of any variety.

If God is a Creator, then God cannot be absolutely pure because Creation consists in part of improving upon one's errors and offering less purchase to one's vices.

What about people—we've all heard about people who die after living lives of greed and misery, rotten people, detestable in every way, but at the last minute, the last few weeks, they call in the priest, they get seraphic smiles on their faces, they have money, perhaps, they're surrounded by servants, and they go off into the Hereafter feeling very good about themselves—deluded, perhaps, about their ultimate worth, but nonetheless smiling, saying their prayers. They haven't gone to a church or done anything decent—

Well, you're creating an improbable person.

There are people like that who die happy after living a miserable life.

Who says they died happy? They could be acting right until the end.

That's the moment you said you don't act.

No. No. I said people who are serious about their deaths don't act. They may be acting for others, but not before eternity.

I'll give you an explanation why a truly rotten person can die happy, which is that they were so rotten in their previous existence, the life before this one, that this life, bad as it was, proved to be a spiritual improvement over the previous one. They die happy because they feel, everything considered—considering how bad were their beginnings and how absolutely loathsome the initial impulses they were born with—that they have, under the circumstances, gotten better than they were before. We all know people who were total pricks their entire lives who mellow a little bit at the end. That's another human quality.

But you said all the good and evil in one's life is summed up in death. I'm thinking of those who are miserable people for the first 95 percent of their lives and then they're sweet old people at the end—doesn't seem very just that they should have a happy death. You'd think somehow they should have a miserable death. Where's the fairness in things?

I think you're speaking too hypothetically. This person you're talking about—as a novelist I find him impossible to draw for a book. People who are rotten all their lives rarely end up sweet at the end. If they do—there is such a thing as truly evil and ugly impulses wearing out, burning out. Just as good people can sour, ugly people may sometimes die in a more benign state. They've used up the ugliness in themselves. They've been rotten, but maybe they feel a bit of contrition at the end. Catholicism is based on that.

Absolutely.

Between the stirrup and the ground. I've always found it excessively sentimental and too easy: Be evil all your life and as you're falling from the horse, before your head is knocked off your body—

Say a perfect Act of Contrition!

Yes! I've always found that extreme—and a little convenient. The Catholic Church is a study not only in immense human wisdom but of applied skill at maneuvering our thoughts around the most nonnavigable corners.

It's thought of almost everything. It has an answer for almost everything, every issue.

You spoke a little bit about Limbo, but I don't recall that you said much about Purgatory—as an idea, as a place, as a metaphor. Of course, it's a wonderful metaphor, we all use it. What is your idea of Purgatory as a metaphor?

Well, as a metaphor—tell me, Purgatory is a temporary station?

It may last for a millennium, but it's temporary.

I confess I don't know these concepts past a few superficial notions. Does Limbo have any relation to Purgatory?

No. Limbo is the place for those people on whom God can't make a judgment. They died before they were baptized.

Absolutely meaningless. Silly.

I agree. The Church doesn't even talk about Limbo anymore. They've almost dropped it as a concept. But Purgatory . . .

Now, Purgatory . . . yes.

Purgatory is not endless. There is an end to your suffering. The amount of time you're there and what kind of suffering you have, according to the Catholic Church, depends on what your crimes were.

I see Purgatory in different terms. In place of the notion that if you suffer long enough you'll purge yourself, I would suggest that being reborn takes care of Purgatory. For some people, life is Purgatory, all-but-endless suffering. And for a few people, life is Heaven—they're happy much of the time. For most people, life can be an intermittent Hell. I don't think we need other structures. I think our debts are paid by way of our reincarnations. That makes more sense to me than supporting those immensely wasteful estates called Heaven and Hell, where nobody does anything, where nothing's brought back into the divine economy, and people just mark time.

I see God as Faustian, as aiming to go farther. God is not satisfied with His or Her Creation. God wants the Creation to become better. Therefore, wasteful procedures are anathemas to God. And so, I do see Heaven, Purgatory, and Hell as wasteful institutions. Who can speak interestingly of Heaven, after all? Shaw made the best single attempt and decided Heaven was boring. And there is always the uneasy little feeling that people have that it could be like Club Med, a gated little tropical island. Whereas on earth, in life, we do experience Heaven. We experience it two, three, or four times in a long life, maybe for a minute, no more, but we know what Heaven is. There's a kind of luminousness to the joy. Most of us, unfortunately, come closest to Heaven through drugs. But, all right—we know what it is.

We certainly know what Hell is. Hell can be as simple as having a bad case of gout. Or a screamer of a drug trip. Or a nerve gone crazy in a tooth.

There's conscience....

Yes, indeed. There's also dread. When we feel dread, we may not be that far from Purgatory. Something important could be taking place in our soul, but we don't know what. We are full of fear at taking the next step, which we now believe is demanded of us. Most men encounter dread in terms of their personal courage. If they're afraid—if they're afraid of playing football—putting on the pads and going out to play can be Purgatory. Boxing can be Purgatory. Skiing, if the trail is steep and narrow and the moguls are formidable, can certainly reduce you. I've never done it, but I would suppose bungee jumping can be Purgatory—brief but intense. Men and women are beginning to search for such living ventures into Purgatory. It used to be that women's Purgatory was related to the terrors of childbirth. After all, in the Middle Ages, there was one chance in ten a woman would die in childbirth. That was a true terror. One had to face ultimates to have a child.

If you've been bad but not so bad that you should be condemned to eternal hellfire—you've only been sort *of bad—the Church said, "You're right, we have a place for those people where they have modest suffering." Then people said, "What about people outside the Church? We've been told they're condemned, but what if they haven't done anything evil? They died at three years old—a wonderful little child but never baptized." The Church said, "We*

have a place for them, too." So the Church was trying to create—
I'm sure they would have created another place if they'd had to. But
ultimately, the Church began to see the folly of Limbo—what a
ridiculous idea for people to live in a big, empty space forever and
feel no positive pain but no positive joy, although the Baltimore
Catechism decided to offer these innocents "perfect natural happi-
ness." No beatific vision would be available but no unseemly suffer-
ing either, just Limbo.

We talked about saints, but I never got to my question about
demons. I remember you told me some time ago you had an en-
counter with a demon—or a succubus or whatever you want to call
it—right here in a room you rented for a week one winter on Com-
mercial Street in Provincetown. Would it be worthwhile to say any-
thing about that experience?

I won't get into it, Mike, because it takes too long to tell,
and there's no real point. I can certainly speak of succubi and
incubi in the abstract sense. I think they would be useful instruments of the Devil. I felt such a presence only once in my
life, and it seemed to come out of nowhere, which is why I
don't rush to talk about it because I don't understand why it
was there. But I really felt as if there were some intangible
creature fastened to my chest even as I was trying to sleep. It
suggests a story that may be worth telling about a poetess
named Mina Loy. Something like seventy or seventy-five
years ago, she was staying in a small hotel on the Left Bank in
Paris, and one night in her room, she felt this hideous oppres-
sion, this monstrous, intangible creature, which seemed
nonetheless most alive and had fastened itself to her chest.
She lived in horror through the night and felt abominably

wretched in the morning. To recover a bit, she went down-stairs to take a coffee on the terrace of the little hotel she was staying at, just across the street from the Seine. Aleister Crowley, the famous and notorious magician, was there, a table or two away, and was talking about a man he detested who was also staying at the hotel. And Crowley said, "You know, last night I sent an incubus to invade him, yet when I saw him this morning, he looked perfectly all right. I don't understand it." Mina Loy's comment was, "Let no one say Aleister Crowley is without powers. It is just that they are misdirected."

Let me shift to wealth and poverty. In the last interview we did, you never addressed this. Are wealth and poverty predetermined by what God gives you when you're born? And how much would you say comes from the accidents of the economic jungle?

The poor often believe they are going to be rewarded in the next life. The wealthy also believe—a good many of them at any rate—that they, too, are going to be rewarded. The Egyptians, for example, believed you had no chance whatso-ever in the Hereafter unless you were truly wealthy. You had to be buried in such a way that all preparations had been made by your family to enable you to travel safely through the underworld long enough to reach their heaven, the Elysian fields. For that, you needed varieties of protection. Priests had to pray for you, amulets were sewn onto your bur-ial garments, you were in need of prayers recited by your rel-atives, and, most of all, you needed a tomb to protect you from evil spirits whenever you needed rest—you would go out and explore the underworld and then come back to your tomb, where your spirit would enter again into your embalmed mummy, which rested, of course, in your highly decorated and protective casket. After some rest, you would again go out into the underworld for another reconnaissance. Finally, you might make it through. Sometimes you didn't. Rich Egyptians used to have a prayer: "Oh, Amon, do not let me die a second time in the Land of the Dead." The Egyptians believed that the second death was final. The first was provisional, but if you were able to find a way through the underworld into the Elysian fields, you could live forever. So, for them, wealth was crucial. A poor man without the protection of priests, amulets, and a tomb had no chance at all— which may be why we still have that long-lived phenomenon of an early civilization: to wit, most people live at a subsistence level, but there is fabulous wealth at the top, and the rich certainly know how to protect it.

I think that belief does carry over. People who are abstemious might look with horror on rich people who have gold plates under the serving dishes for dinner. But the rich obviously believe that the afterworld is structured to enable people who are rich to have more of a purchase on eternity. Not all rich people—some rich people feel guilty. Late in life, they pursue philanthropy—they're terrified of the Hereafter. They know what they did to get that wealth, and they are in terror.

Then some of the poor—some who are bitter and furious—feel they were absolutely denied any chance at future existence. They are very angry at God. You also have the poor who believe that it's right and fair. I've lived a clean life, a good life, I've raised my children, done my best, I've never despaired, and I'm going to go to a good place.

We have these separate outlooks, and we have an ongoing question for those who believe in a continuance after death. At a guess—my guess—I would think there's constant negotiation between God and the Devil over who travels where. I'm assuming that not only is God not All-Powerful, but neither is the Devil. The two remain in deep contest with each other. The Devil, therefore, would not wish to be excluded completely from the possibility of rebirth. The Devil might desire to have some of His rich people taken care of. Of course, there are rich people who are close to saintly, who manage to live with their wealth in such a way that it hasn't corrupted them. I think that's rare—but it does occur; we've all known a few. They are lovely people sometimes. Not all rich people are awful, but a great many rich people are certainly in no shape to pass through the eye of the needle. Nonetheless, you can find a lively energy in some of the rich. Some of them made their money, after all, through their huge energy or by way of their audacity. Not all people who gain power arrive through foul means alone.

So I expect God to be perfectly willing to discriminate. Certain of the rich, yes, absolutely, let's send them out to be born again. They're interesting.

Are you saying that God will endow some to be born again into great wealth? Or into poverty?

Yes. Why not? It's a species of testing. People who were born in rich and favorable circumstances in one life and grew

spoiled and had lives that proved disappointing to His anticipa-
tions might be reborn as poor people. Others who were poor
but never turned bitter or felt that they were deprived might be
rewarded—a dubious reward is wealth, for that is always full of
tests. But then some of the poor had a touch of aristocracy in-
nate in them. And there are rich people who have the modesty
of poor people. One function of reincarnation may be to give
God further insights into us. I go back to the fundamental
premise: God does not understand us completely any more
than we understand our children. We can know them well in
terms of their habits, some of their virtues, and some of their
faults, but we certainly don't understand them altogether. So
God wants to know more about His Creation, whereas the
Devil is attempting to muck up precisely that clarity.

*I don't have any disputes on the individual level, but when I think
of that phrase of Adam Smith's, "the wealth of nations," there are
some peoples, some nations, who have lived in terrible, terrible misery. Take one people I know a little about, the Irish. For five hundred, six hundred years they lived under British wealth and power,
and now it seems just that the Irish are richer than the English.
They're now the wealthiest nation in the European Union.*

I'll give you another example. For a thousand years and
more, the Jews lived in the ghetto. In most countries, they
weren't allowed to hunt or fish or farm; they were allowed to
be moneylenders or innkeepers or to own shops in their own
communities. So what did they do? They gave everything
they had to their schools. I would say that the results got into
the gene stream—those ghetto Jews put their emphasis on

learning and intelligence because their own books, particularly the Talmud, happened to be all that was open to them.

But if you look at all the plusses and minuses of all the nations—great wealth in some and great poverty in others—how does that mesh with the individual decisions that God and the Devil express by way of reincarnation? It seems God may have to give up a whole country or a whole race of people for long periods.

I don't want to get carried away with understanding God's motives. I'm looking to find a few general principles.

You're looking at individuals. I'm asking you to look at it from a national point of view.

That means first you have to believe in races. I do, to a certain extent. It's completely incorrect these days to talk about such matters, but I think the specific mixture of climate and language over many centuries does produce one kind of person as opposed to another. That may now be part of God's interest in us as individuals: "Will this particular man or woman turn out better or worse than I think he or she will?" God's also interested in races—how will they turn out?

In nations.

Yes, as nations. But that is far more complicated.

God must be thinking a lot about China, with one billion–plus people.

God learns. I keep coming back to my fundamental mnemonic—God learns. This is why I'm so opposed to those

religions which assume that God is in command of everything.

*Last time we spoke, you said that God was developing evolution as
He went along.*
   Yes. God learns.

*Then in those early periods of time, when land had just been cre-
ated, you indicated that God was in the slime of early Creation, yes,
in there evolving with everything else. Yet you also said with great
assurance that God is the Creator of the world and the solar system.
I have trouble reconciling God-in-the-slime and God-as-Creator—*
   Suppose God is the lord of the solar system but at the
same time had to learn how to develop the system from the
slime on up.

Yes, but when did God put the souls into Creation?
   The key to the notion is that it's all been a huge experiment, an ongoing, developing experiment with countless results, good and bad, but most of them were good enough so
that evolution continued despite its failures. God learns. And
so God invests Himself or Herself in all sorts of creatures en
route—not only animals but flora as well.
   Once again, I don't subscribe to the iron declarations of
the Old Testament and the New Testament. Both were written by committee. The Old Testament was put together over
a long period by a series of very talented committees, much
more talented than the latter-day Bible builders who composed the New Testament. On the other hand, the people

who wrote the New Testament were good enough scholars to be familiar with the best remarks that had been made up to that point in the Old Testament and by many a sage, prophet, and mystic. So they used that as well. They were also attached to a concept that may or may not be true, which is that Jesus was the son of God. They were serious men, but they were also a committee. So as literary works, the Old Testament has some faults, and the New Testament a good many. But to accept them as the absolute map of our spiritual universe is comparable to using the kind of charts Christopher Columbus had to look at before he set out for the West. For instance, even our current idea of the Beginning, as it is presented in English in the first three sentences of Genesis, is a false concept.

In fact, one summer I studied classical Hebrew on my own, and the first sentence of Genesis—have we discussed that?

No.

Well, as you know: "In the beginning, God created the heavens and the earth." Or so it goes in English. Actually, the first word of the Old Testament—in the original—is most singular. It's only existence is as the first word of the Old Testament, "*barashith*." The second word is "*bora*." There are many interpretations of "*barashith*," but I came up with "out of the pits" or "out of the depths." "*Bora*" is "being" or "creating." So the first two words might say, "out of the depths came being." The next words are not "the heavens and the earth" but "the firmament above" and "the firmament below," as if to declare that there are two species of existence out there from the commencement. And then the next sentence? "The breath of God moved upon the waters"—

"The breath of God upon the waters."

It's not "breath of God" at all. The word used here for breath is *"ruach."* In classical Hebrew, there are three varieties of breath to signify God's presence. There's *"ruach,"* *"nefesh,"* and *"neshamah."* *"Neshamah,"* if I recall correctly, is the gentle breath. And *"nefesh"* is a normal wind. *"Ruach"* is the fierce breath, the angry breath, God's rage. So the line really says, "and the rage of God roared over the waters." So to go back, the first two sentences can well be translated as, "Out of the depths came being, and God created the firmament above and the firmament below. And God's fierce breath roared over the waters."

Much different.

Yes, I'm suspicious of committees. Even the great one that gave us the King James Bible.

We've spoken a bit about technology. I'd like to go back to that. Most of humanity sees technology as a way to free us from drudgery and give us leisure time to read and think and travel, and so forth. Why shouldn't it be seen on balance, on balance—I understand all the bad things about it, but why shouldn't technology be seen as largely salutary?

I have four words to describe technology, which I've used several times now: more power, less pleasure. I think there's no getting around it: We can't pretend more pleasure comes to us from technology. It tends to crimp our senses and reduce us to people who are able to live in a closed environment. My notion—it's a sentimental notion, doubtless—is that God would have preferred us to be able to do the things we now achieve through technology by means of our spirit alone. In other words, instead of having television, we could reach into our dream life and enjoy organized and marvelous dramas that we could create for ourselves or send by telepathy to our friends. The ultimate aim was for every human being to be immensely creative. Being psychic as well, we would not have needed electronic communications. If I wanted to talk to you, I would be able to put my mind in contact with yours, even if you were in a far-off place. We all have small intimations of that possibility. It seems to me such mental powers are grievously reduced with every advance in technology.

As a specific example, I now use hearing aids, and I can't hear without them, not with most people. But my own small remaining ability to hear gets reduced further by using these hearing aids. In parallel, I think technology tends to curtail our possibilities and accelerate our dependencies.

After all, the great strides that have been made in technology came from previous generations. Maxwell discovered some of the differences between electricity and magnetism. He and Faraday took imaginative, metaphorical leaps. Abraham Lincoln and Winston Churchill didn't have to study previous speeches to come up with the Gettysburg Address or "I have nothing to offer but blood, toil, tears, and sweat."

They came out of a past that depended on independent human beings rising up to exceptional thoughts at incredible moments. They were not dependent on electronic machines they did not really understand. As a small example, I don't know anyone with a computer who doesn't talk about the glitches.

Look, the first person to use a wheel after the drudgery of dragging things must have felt great pleasure. I don't see—

Wait a moment; there are crucial turning points in the advent of modern technology. The center of all that is electronics, whereas the first wheel was made of wood, and sharp stones were used to shape it. These were things people could comprehend, they came out of the earth. Then people began to learn how to smelt ore. Dangerous business, tricky, but they found the means to get fire to melt the ore and so could separate the slag from the molten metal. The Iron Age began.

I say there's a profound difference between early and later technology. Early technology, lasting through to the nineteenth century, consisted of dealing with very powerful and explosive elements in nature and mastering them, so there was awe and excitement to it. Huge excitement for the railroad when it was developed—people loved to travel on trains. They might be cramped and reek of their own foul coal smoke, but they were exciting. Now, traveling on airplanes is not agreeable. Everyone thought it'd be immensely exciting, but it isn't. It's reductive. You don't feel like a voyager so much as a piece of trussed-up, transported goods. Electronics is the great divide—the watershed between what I would call good technology and bad. Because no one knows what electronics is. I defy a physicist to reach my mind with an explanation I can comprehend. For that matter, we don't even know what electricity is. A current of electrons, yes, but do we know anything about the makeup of an electron? Does it possess its own consciousness, or does it not?

So that's the pivot point, then? That's when technology becomes a miserable activity? But when you were a boy, the radio—you must remember the radio, the crystal set and all that.

You had to be able to solder, yes. But even then, you had to buy your vacuum tubes. People assemble computers today out of factory parts. I did model airplanes when they were made of balsa with glue. Then plastic came along. In my childhood, plastic was not common. Bakelite was the nearest you got to it. Now plastic is omnipresent. And it's inert. It doesn't bring on any sense of the uncanny. It offers an inkling of nonexistence. I'm just paranoid enough to believe it's the Devil who loves plastic because it's going to deaden God's sensibilities before it's all over. God won't be able to get to us through shields of plastic. About the time, oh, thirty years ago when women began to wear plastic clothing—the stuff stank, you remember, the awful smell of plastic clothes?—I began to think that may be the point where the ballgame was lost. Women, with their finer sensibilities, were adopting plastic.

My last question: Great religious ideas have great followings, and they last for millennia—some do fade, some die, but the greatest last for millennia. And I'm assuming there's a reason for that. Your faith in the theological and intellectual efficacy of your system is strong. I've observed it for many years, and it's deep-rooted inside you. But you have also said your system is not going to be adopted by many other people.

Not in a hurry. No. There's no immediate solace offered for our fears, only an appeal to our human pride.

Does this bother you?

I suppose that if I had developed these ideas when I was thirty or forty, I would have wanted to become a religious leader. But that is not in my capacity. If there's any validity to any of these thoughts, if they take root in people to some extent, then, yes, these notions may yet be adopted by some. Because I do believe that there are two elements now on the horizon that can yet destroy the world as we know it. One of them is technology and the other is organized religion. The second drives people into stupidity. It can take intelligent children and deprive them of their ability to look at existence. They're obliged to force their thoughts to fit a mold that may never have existed and certainly doesn't exist now. That drives people to extremes. So I do feel that my existential sense of God as a Being who needs us as much as we need Him could yet reach many. But I feel no inner directive to convince people right away. I am just centered enough to recognize how far that is beyond my means.

VI

Ritual and Telepathy

MICHAEL LENNON: *We have not spoken of ritual as part of religion. Recently, my wife and I went to the ordination of an Episcopal priest. It was an extraordinary event. Thirty or forty priests and bishops and deacons stood over the kneeling aspirant, touching a shoulder or back—or, if they could not reach the person, they touched the shoulder of someone who could. All the while, a chorus in the background was chanting "Veni, Sancte Spiritu, Veni, Sancte Spiritu" (Come, Holy Ghost), while another singer, the lead singer, was singing a cappella verses about the glories of being a priest, of the holy responsibilities and obligations, the special status that a priest has among believers, ending with the ancient pronouncement from the ordaining bishop, "Thou art a priest forever." It was a very moving, very powerful experience. It made me think of one of our earlier conversations in which you noted that Funda-*

mentalists believe that if they keep their noses clean and observe rit-
ual, they have a ticket to Heaven. Does ritual have any significant
merit for you, or do you reject it completely?

NORMAN MAILER: I've thought about it a good deal. Put it this
way: I have high suspicions about ritual. It seems to me that
at best, it's a mixed blessing. You know, one of my favorite remarks is that repetition kills the soul. Well, obviously that
remark has to be explored before we go further. Any number
of kinds of repetition are, I will admit, crucial to the human
venture. It is, after all, one of the ways by which we learn. And
there is such a thing as creative repetition. Nonetheless, I'm
suspicious of ritual. Where, after all, does my theology start?
What occasions it? What stimulates it? I would answer that it
is because I have worked as a novelist all my life. I don't want
this to be misunderstood, but, in a certain sense, novelists are
dealing with a few of God's problems—judgment, particularly. If you're any good at your work, you've spent your life
thinking about human nature. Since few good novels can do
without a villain, you are, of course, soon living with the notion of Evil.

Now, where in all this is the relation to ritual? Ritual is
repetition, and in writing a novel you look to do the opposite.
A fine novel does not keep repeating itself. That is exactly the
hallmark of a dull work. So most good novelists are wary of
repetition. Moreover, most people I don't approve of tend to
be masters or monsters of mediocre repetition. The politi-
cians we despise are one example. So one develops an understanding that repetition can be dangerous when used as a tool

for mediocre purposes. Unimaginative parents often know nothing better than to repeat what they say over and over. I confess that worries me about the nature of ritual. I think it looks to set human nature into a form. TV evangelists seem diabolically inspired to me when they cleave and cling to rep-etition. Earlier, as a child, synagogue services left me bored. Most of it washed over me. I might just as well have been a shell on the surf's edge. But for a little wear and tear, I was the same shell at the end of the service as at the beginning, and this was true year after year.

I did experience one ritual that was interesting to me. It was my induction into Transcendental Meditation, which was in fashion thirty-five years ago. I remember that for my initi-ation ceremony, I was told to bring a flower to the initiator. He happened to be a gawky kid who was absolutely wild about Transcendental Meditation, which I had found no more than odd and a little boring. At the commencement of the practice each day, you were supposed to empty your head for twenty minutes. You did your best not to allow much thought to come through. I said to myself, "I've been doing this for years as a writer." Every time one goes to work in the morning, the first thing to do is empty your head. I've been practicing Transcendental Meditation willy-nilly.

Now, during my initiatory ritual, they said a few words in an Asian language and then gave me a mnemonic to repeat. I forget what it was. It was something like Allen Ginsberg's old "OMMMMM." I kept repeating whatever the sound was in my head for twenty minutes. Whenever an errant thought came into my brain, I had to be ready to use the mnemonic to wash the thought away. It was a small ritual, but I did feel an effect. Something did take place. Obviously, then, in a deep and powerful ritual, a great deal happens. Let me move forward to make the point. Given my fundamental notion that God and the Devil are at war all the time, I would go so far as to suggest that ritual may well have been first created by the Devil. God, recognizing its efficacy, and determined not to lose any soul unnecessarily, entered ritual as well. I think ritual is composed then of the presence of God and the Devil. It does tend to have the demons and the saints marching in. There is a power to the repetitions—the music, the chanting, the ceremony, the concentration of the principals. So it may indeed be an important moment. One of my favorite notions is that the Lord and Satan are there when major events occur. A general, on the eve of a great battle, gets out of bed and finds it very important whether he stretches out his left foot first or his right.

A ritual?

No, but he has a sense that powers are present. Anyone who reads Homer will find nothing strange about this. So I think my answer would be that I don't scoff at ritual, but I don't trust it. I would be happier if we lived without it, yet I have to recognize that my upbringing, my tastes, my life have had little to do with rituals. Nonetheless, they are fascinating. Because there may be any number of occasions when God and the Devil have to cooperate—exactly because they each are trying to outwit the other. For that, they have, at times, to engage in formal contact. Wrestlers do have to grasp each other.

What about rituals concerning athletes? I'm sure professional boxers decide which glove is going to be laced on first, and how many minutes they want to be alone before the fight, and which jockstrap they will wear. I know professional baseball players have certain things they have to do. The center fielder has to step on second base when he runs in or, you know, the forces will be against him. So athletes are particularly superstitious, and they go through various rituals and preparations before and during the game. Soldiers do the same thing. When I was in the navy, I knew sailors who were tremendously ritualistic about how they tied a knot. It was a bad omen if you tied a knot the wrong way, or if something on the ship was not performed in exactly the right way. You felt like you were calling down evil things upon you. These are not religious rituals, but they are often done with the knowledge that there is something in the air.

Yes. I used to be susceptible to that when I was younger. I do know what you are talking about. Back in San Francisco, in 1963, I used to walk parapets which had sheer drops to the street below. (I felt as if it was an imperative from my soul to take such a chance.) I used to be full of dread every morning because I knew that before the day was done, I'd be walking a parapet. They varied between eight inches in width to so much as a foot and a half, so there was no great risk unless you lost your head. But I would suspect that the spirit world, if you will, does pay close attention to people engaged in unusual events. We started by talking about ritual. Now we are involved with rote. Whenever people engage in rote—in other words, express a superstitious fear by going in for repetitive moves when a good deal is at stake—that can draw the attention of the gods. So athletes who are going to be playing in games that will have a large emotional effect on many people are going to attract such attention. I think many have the feeling that one is not alone but is among accompanying spirits. At the least!

I never told you this story, but when I was writing my doctoral thesis on you, I had a chapter on your cosmology. I had to face two or three English professors plus a philosophy professor on the Ph.D. committee. He argued with me about it. Wrote me long letters.

Let me get this straight. While you were formulating the thesis, this happened?

Yes, he was reading drafts. He said that your system, as far as he could understand it, was terribly incomplete.

[N.M. laughs]

He said he could not find in it either a beginning, how the universe came into being, or how it ends—how the cosmic war would end at the end of time or even if there would be an end of time.

He sounds like a major-league ass.

Well, no, he was gentle with me. But he thought anybody who had a philosophical system, ought to have—let me finish—

Let me just stress one point: I've never heard of this before, that you have to have a beginning and an end to your philosophy. What about Logical Positivists? Do they have a beginning and an end?

Well, he was an Aristotelian. That probably explains a lot. But he also felt that you had no clear definition of Being—what he believed and what a lot of philosophers believe is the central question of philosophy: Being. What is Being? What is the ultimate nature of man? What is the ultimate nature of God? What is Being? When he confronted me, I kept saying existentialism, existentialism—as much as I knew about it, and I knew a little but not a great deal. One of my English professors on the committee said, "Look, Mailer is a literary man. He's not a systematic philosopher. He has ideas, he has feelings, but he isn't out to create a philosophical system." And that's what finally got the philosopher to back down. He goes, "You're right. This is a literature Ph.D., not a philosophy Ph.D." After all, you have written about Marx, Freud, Kierkegaard, Sartre, Schopenhauer—it wasn't that you weren't familiar with some philosophy; you were clearly interested in philosophical questions. But finally, I guess, any philosopher who won't propose any ultimates is a very unusual philosopher. As I read it, you present no ultimate nature of God, no ultimate answer to any of these questions. And so, reading over everything that we have done so far, I keep coming to the same thing—we don't know, we can't be certain. Yet from most philosophical points of view, there's usually one rock somewhere.

What if the rock is in transit? In other words, when we say "rock," we mean something that is eternal. What if eternity is in passage itself? The simplest response I could give is that no philosopher has ever come up with an answer to these questions that is satisfactory to us. No human, and I won't be the first either. What I will say is this. I have basic beliefs. I don't know what we've been talking about through these interviews. I thought I'd said it. God is not All-Powerful and not All-Good. God is comparable to a Greek god if you will— Zeus, if we need some model. I don't need one. In other words, God is a divine protagonist engaged in trying to shape some very large part of existence. How large is a question beyond our means. Of course! I have no notion at all whether our God is only a master of the solar system or commands galaxies. I have no notion whether God is in command of black holes in space or is terrified of them. My fundamental idea is that the cosmos is at war within itself and the God who created us is not the Emperor, but the Artist. This is my most basic notion: God—Being, if you will—is not a lawgiver but an artist. Being is doing the best that He or She can do to project a new notion of existence into the cosmos. There may be other notions out there as well—other concepts concerning which turn the cosmos should take. We humans are part of God's venture into the unknown. We humans are God's soldiers, God's ability to change the given in the cosmos. To ask, then, that the end be posited is philosophically misleading, since we commence with the notion that the end is as yet undetermined.

When I say that I am an existentialist, I mean that the purpose of existence is not known. It is the presence of life, not the definitive of it. God may often dwell in states of bewilderment. That makes more sense to me than that God knows clearly what He or She is doing and tells us how to do it. If that is the case, we are no more than extras in a huge opera. I've said this over and over. The end is open. Existence is open. The notion that there is a predetermined place we all will reach, that there is a single point to existence that we will achieve by fulfilling God's notion is, if you stop to think, no more than a personification of God as the director of an immense opera. There He stands, holding his full libretto in mind. But I am saying it is more complex, more difficult, more ennobling. And the libretto is not done. It is still being written. We are not just serfs, nor children drawn in to sing in the chorus. We are the base of this opera. So to demand a philosophical presentation where I must say where we are going is, given my point of view, not an answerable demand. All we can know, at best, is where we might be at the present. Everything in existence fortifies this concept for me. I know where I am at this moment, within reason. But do I know where I will be in a year? Will I still be alive? I don't know. If I should remain alive for twenty years, can I have any notion of how I will be then? Can I have a concept of where society will find itself in a hundred years? Hardly. We live in the present. That is what we are given. We do have instincts, and they can be far-reaching. I would go so far as to say that I would go along with Goethe's belief that these powerful instincts are God given. We are embodying God's plans, but such plans are subject to change because the storms of the cosmos are not all prerecorded; the future of the world is not yet written. The Devil, after all, warps human affairs.

Here I wish to enter a relevant note. The moment of death carries more weight in your theological thinking than in any other I know of, but I don't see any consideration of what happens to those, I believe it's 20 percent of all people, who die of strokes, heart attacks, aneurysms. I have a friend who died, so the doctor said, before he hit the ground—you know, there is no time for them to prepare themselves, there is no time to reflect, project, anything. Are they just unlucky? Is this just a flaw in the way God did things, given the importance of our state of mind when we go into eternity? These people have no chance.

The answer may lie in the famous Catholic dictum with which Graham Greene was obsessed: There is always time to repent! Between the stirrup and the ground! Time, after all, as anyone who has had experience with minor drugs like marijuana will know, can extend or compress. A tenth of a second in a dream, we are told, can feel like five minutes. But apart from that, even if you have no time at the moment before your death, I would say that death takes place within us as we live our lives. The recognition of death is always posing the question, "Am I a good man or a bad man?" that accompanies us from an early age. "Am I a good child or a bad child?" As you grow older, you also think more about judgment. Of course, not everyone believes that such a process exists. It is disheartening that so often you will hear fine people say, "Oh, there is nothing after this. All I want is a little peace." It is a sad remark, particularly sad to me because, given my notion that many of us look to the promise of being reborn, it is sad if life has been so corrosive that one does not care to be rein-

carnated. That suggests there has been too punishing an existence, too deep a sense of defeat.

*I'm not making myself sufficiently clear. We had a long discussion in
which you emphasized how critical the final moments of one's life
were. They were, according to you, extraordinarily important because that was the time to prepare yourself. You used the example of
people in the gas chambers who were cheated out of that moment
and how terrible it was for them. But, you know, if you have a
brain aneurysm, you don't have a tenth of a second. You have nothing. Your brain stops. There's no thought.*

Let's say 99 percent of the people who are alive have a reasonable amount of time to think before they die.

They do.

All right. You are talking about the 1 percent who don't.
And if I can't account for that 1 percent, then I can't. Everything I attempt here, if I may honor it with the assumption
that it is philosophical, suggests that we don't look for 100
percent in anything. I'm opposed to the notion that any kind
of thought can be wholly complete once it looks to engage
the meaning of life. That is another reason for detesting Fundamentalism. It insists on 100 percent. What I have to say
may be valid only for some people, but I do believe that, yes,
our preparation for death is important. If you have just a few
minutes at the end, it isn't as if you are facing death for the
first time; you have been facing it all your life. Let us say you
are handing in the final submission.

Now, let me go back a moment. As I've indicated, I think reincarnation is a species of reward. To repeat, that's why I get depressed when people say, "Oh, I just want some peace," and mean it—whereas others can feel that with all the ill they've admittedly caused there is still enough good in them to want another chance. I believe God is ready to give that chance to the most impossible cases. I go back to my basic notion: God is our Artist. A fine artist is never satisfied with what has been created but looks for another attempt to do better. I even believe that the dullest human is still an intrinsic work of art. It is just that virtually none of the potential was realized. Still, there may be some reason for the Creator to wish to see if this human can improve.

God needs us. To repeat: He wishes to take His notion of existence and carry it across the stars. And for that, God needs humans to become more extraordinary. But you don't create people who are wonderful by an act of will. Often, such development can come only from rebirth and endless small steps of change. If you are put in situations where you failed in one life but manage to succeed in the next, then, yes, to that degree, you have strengthened God.

Let me offer a crude scenario. If, in one existence, you were terrified of heights, well, then, possibly for the next you are placed in a family of mountain climbers. So as a child in this new existence, you may go through horrors. But now you have guides to carry you up to an aerie you could not reach in your previous life.

So I would venture to say that at the moment of one's

death, one may have a better sense of what one did or didn't do in one's life and what one might like for the next life. Can that not give a coloration to the soul even at the last moment?

All right. Let us say that such a person does become a successful mountain climber. If you have a succession of such good reincarnations, what happens then? Does a person ever get to be as good as it is possible to become?

I don't think so. Most of us are so highly imperfect, so underdeveloped, so frustrated, so small in relation to what we could have been—every one of us, even those of us who are relatively successful—that the question also becomes: How much has God learned from us? It isn't that God understands us so well that all we need is a little tweaking. God learns along with us. Continue to think of God as a protagonist in the cosmos. So, some of His divine decisions on reincarnation will work; others not. God's hope is that His works succeed more than they fail.

So most reincarnations might not show a clear improvement?

Who knows? Karma itself may be embattled. When too many people die at once—when a hundred thousand souls living in Hiroshima are incinerated in one second—that may create incalculable damage. Karma may not have been equipped to deal with so many deaths in one instant. Might this not be one of the Devil's most profound urges? To maim karma irreparably? Destroy reincarnation, which is to say, destroy God's way of adjusting the balance?

I don't see any reason why reincarnations can't go on for a couple of
million years. Why not? No problem.

The question here is, How much time does God have? Are
eons available, or is it a cosmic race? There may be other visions of existence seeking to overtake us in the universe—or,
worse, speed far away from us. So God may be in a great
hurry. God may have less patience now than He possessed
hundreds of thousands of years ago.

Well, to go back to my philosophy professor, there is usually some
teleological sense among philosophers about how it's going to turn
out in the end.

I would say that God has a vision of existence that He sees
as more creative and more useful to the future than other
competing visions in the cosmos.

What is that vision?

That life can become more and more creative, diverse,
splendid, and incredible.

Okay.

Now give me another vision of existence. That we all are
to sit in the heavenly fold and listen to hymns that are beautiful because God has put us in Heaven? What the hell is
more final about that?

There is the vision in many religions that you merge with the uni-
versal mind. You merge with the mind of God, you become part and
parcel of God. And you do not just exist in sugar land or Club Med

but exist in pure intellectual bliss, having been completely purged of all weaknesses and corruptions and so forth. Many religions hold this belief. The Hindus, for example.

That assumes we're all here, ideally, to get to a certain place. If we keep our lives pure enough, we will reach such bliss. But I am saying that heavenly bliss is not guaranteed. Everything we know about the nature of existence also shows us that it's cruel, paradoxical, glorious, disappointing, tremendous, and often more modest than we expected. And so I believe we are part of a vast creative process that is attempting to go somewhere without being able to guarantee what the end is. In our lives, we certainly work without knowing the end. The only certainty we possess is that we are going to die. We don't know what will follow that. We can assume certain answers, but we know, or ought to know, that we are making no more than an assumption. Let me add that if every one of our understandings comes down to uncertainty, why assume that God knows what the end is? That is also a large assumption.

Does it fit or not fit in your theology that America has a special place in God's vision?

I've written about that on occasion. The quagmire in Iraq can be blamed on American Exceptionalism. I would say that all of us, all humans, belong to exceptionalism—not just Americans. All of the globe is part of God's exceptionalism. It's vainglory to think we Americans have sole purchase on it. How, for God's sakes, could God put up with suburbs and malls and superhighways and plastics?

Well, maybe we've blown it. You know, in the beginning, the idea of American Exceptionalism came from the idea that they blew it in Europe. There were endless wars and corruption. And we were a new start.

I won't argue that there may have been certain divine hopes for America. But I don't think He has had much of that since the Second World War. In the last five decades, we've not only roiled the depths but cheapened the surface of life. We've ruined the freshness of the air, the cleanliness of the rivers, the integrity of the earth. At this point, I would say that America is not a country whose spiritual goodness is guaranteed to hold up under examination.

I know when Kennedy was assassinated somebody said, and you quoted it, that God may have withdrawn His blessing from America.
It was John Updike.

And that remark moved you. You thought he might be onto something there.
Yes.

Several times in this and other conversations I've had with you, you've mentioned the possibility that God might have intended human beings to develop their telepathic powers. In your novel Ancient Evenings *some of the characters do employ exactly such powers. And modern novelists can, in a sense, read minds, because they're exploring what people are thinking. One of the great advances is when the novel moved into the human mind.*
In which century would you say that was?

Well, it really only started around a hundred years ago.

Dickens enters people's minds.

Not much. Not like Joyce. Or Virginia Woolf.

All right.

Do your speculations about telepathy have anything to do with using this novelistic tool? I mean you certainly explore the consciousness of virtually all of your heroes. You rarely see characters from just the outside.

Yes, but I don't think that I would lay claim to any more telepathy than is average. We all have had the experience of thinking of a song and then someone in the room starts humming it. People who are married for a while often find they're thinking of something at the same time. We phone someone just as they are about to call us. But in terms of daily novel writing, I think we study everybody from the outside. Once in a while, through love, we do literally enter the inner presence of someone else. But generally speaking, we novelists observe. We study society. We try to understand how the social machine works. We try to understand characters who are different from ourselves. We work with the notion that there is a little bit of ourselves in the stranger. Certain characters do come alive even though they are far apart from our notion of our self. The best novelists can do that. All the same, telepathy is but a small part of it now. Electronics, I suspect, are the Devil's contribution. God just assumed we would become more and more telepathic, and, in the course of that, there would be less need for technology. Technology stifles

God's creation. Smog is not good for God's air. Static is not good for His ears or ours. I don't want to go through the old litany of all that is wrong with modern civilization. I will add one notion, however, which is that technology now being with us, we have to look upon human history as God's attempt to deal with the Devil as well as with us. If the Devil succeeds in establishing technological shoots and outbursts and venues and avenues throughout all of society, God must engage technology as well. But He comes in second. The Devil is the pioneer in technology. So I would assert, unless it is we humans who outstripped the Devil.

Right. But one of the new phenomena of technology that is sweeping not just the United States but the world—in fact, the United States, I understand, is behind great portions of the development, certainly in Europe and Asia—is cell phones. Only half the people in the States use cell phones, but in Asia and in Europe it's much higher than that. It's 70, 80 percent. Is this opportunity to call up people all the time, anywhere in the world, not creating a whole new set of communications in the world that never existed before?

I see it as the kind of mess that comes from an overreliance on comfort. I'm not at all sure that instant communication with everyone alive is ideal, not at all. In the past, it was often the hunt for information that shaped the development we made of the information. We were stimulated by the hunt. The difficulty in obtaining information was a most vital part of the intellectual process. Today, we talk about gluts of information. We are all being buried under lava flows of data.

I remember you were there at the birth of television, and you had many theories about it and have written about it. It seems to me that the cell phone in many ways is almost equal in its power.

With television, back in the early days, everybody who felt positive about it was leaving the full effect of commercials out of the equation. TV commercials did something wasteful to the American people. They introduced the expectation that your powers of concentration were required to suffer a series of hits (interruptions) through every hour that you watched.

You've made it clear that, to your mind, ideation may be closer to the Devil than the Lord—which made me think, what about language, which is perhaps the most complex and subtle creation of intellect? Where does language fit into this discussion?

Language does not come only from intellect. Language is the marriage of intellect and the senses, whereas technology is often divorced from the latter—plastic, for example. Most electronic machines are not agreeable to employ. Think of the cast-iron vise in an old-fashioned cellar workshop. It makes cranking sounds as you use it, and you do get a feeling as you tighten its iron jaws whether the piece in the vise is being held properly, not being crushed and not too loose. You obtain very little of that with technological machines. Usually you are reading dials, and your eyes might even find a little play in the subtlety of the needle. But you can't ask technology to enrich your physical reactions. Whereas language does come out of the senses. Half of language is onomatopoeia. We are drawn to different languages by their qualities. I love

German for its guttural vibrations on one's larynx and French for the emphasis upon the nose, the centrality of the nose. I love English for the mannered postures available to your voice and Spanish for the fire you can feel within it—ditto for Italian with its sense of bravura, Hebrew for its primitive roots. All such reactions come from our senses. So I separate technology and language—they exist at opposite poles of the intellect.

I've never heard you speak philosophically about language.

Well, I had all sorts of theories years ago, but I never came to grips with it. I do have these notions still. I think certain consonants have associative qualities. I would say that in English, "r" almost always has to do with anger, rage, ire, fury, redness, roar. "L" may be related to love—lassitude, leisure, likelihood, languor, libidos, luxury. "S"s are sibilant. They suggest displeasure, sinuosity. I tried to make up a rule for all the consonants, but "r," "l," and "s" are the easiest. "B" is almost always impact—"b," "k," you know: "break." Sounds that implode upon your ear tend to have relations to "b," "k," "f."

Well, what is the relationship between God and the Devil to language?

That's beyond me. But, look, animals come close to speaking. I had a dog fifty years ago, a standard poodle, immensely bright. I always felt that his greatest pain, his soul-suffering, came from his inability to speak—because dogs, in my opinion, do have souls, and in fact, parenthetically, there is one very large but unascertainable notion that in karma we may go back into the animal chain again. Who can know? In any event, this dog was extraordinary. He made searching sounds in his throat, trying to speak to me, sounds you couldn't begin to spell out. I could make them for the tape recorder, but no one could transcribe them. And that dog wanted to speak. So I think in a certain sense, God was discovering language through the eons of evolution and the sounds of His animals.

All right, here's my last question. Have recent geopolitical events reaffirmed or undercut your theological beliefs? I mean, has the re-election of George Bush confirmed your belief system?

I've felt from the word go that George Bush is one of the Devil's clients. And every time he feels that Jesus is talking to him, count on it: Satan is in his ear. One of the Devil's greatest talents could be to speak like Jesus. The war in Iraq has been steroidal for America. So in that sense, yes—I think the Devil may be winning right now in America. But it's still coming down to the wire.

VII

Intelligent Design

MICHAEL LENNON: *I know you've been thinking about Intelligent Design, and I have, too. But aren't you an unlikely person to find credence there?*

NORMAN MAILER: Why?

Because it's a pet theory of the Fundamentalists.

Novelists can't afford to be ideologically bound, even if, in practice, we are. Many of us do tie ourselves up by way of style. Take Henry James or Hemingway. Both were fabulous stylists, but they paid for that huge achievement by being able to write only about certain matters. Their style locked them into narrower modes of perception. As I've said often enough, Picasso had a huge influence on me. For him, style was not a part of one's person but a tool to use for making a particular attack on reality—different tools for engaging different kinds of complex reality.

This said, let me admit that I come to the question of Intelligent Design with, once again, no great cognizance of the subject. On the other hand, the premise behind these interviews is that I won't be embarrassed by my lack of knowledge. Theologians—no matter at what high level they cerebrate—are trapped, as I have suggested, by their already-received religious systems. They are obliged to do their thinking with ideas they are not all that free to change. So theologians build the innovations in their philosophies by way of mental gymnastics, particularly when it comes to All-Good and All-Powerful. And, no surprise, they avoid many questions they cannot begin to confront.

The recent tsunami comes to mind. What was offered for explanation by religious spokesmen was that God is a great mystery. His ways are unfathomable. One more time, they were hiding behind the Mystery.

As is obvious from these interviews, my feeling is that God strives to find a better, more well-adapted creation than His latest design. Remember my earlier remark that the dinosaurs, at one point, may have been a large part of God's élan. He had dared to create this immense animal who might be able to rule the jungles, the mountains, and the plains. Then, He came to discover that He had misdesigned it. Back to the drawing board. God, like us, makes mistakes. I must say that if Intelligent Design is being welcomed by Fundamentalists, they are asking for considerable trouble in the future.

Well, I don't want to say they invented the idea. It's been around since the eighteenth century, when the world was conceived to be virtually a clock, it was so perfectly designed. Intelligent Design grows out of the Enlightenment.

Perhaps I have a misunderstanding of what is meant by Intelligent Design. I can only speak of it on the basis of my own comprehension. Does it not offer the notion that there is an element in existence that occasionally inserts a more advanced design into an ongoing evolution? I do deem this to be apt for what I am talking about. Because, yes, I do think that God is always looking to make existence better, more finely designed. And in corollary to that, God looks to improve on His errors.

Can't you see how such ideas can lend support to people opposed to evolution? Intelligent Design shows the hand of the Creator.

Yes, but that doesn't make Him an All-Powerful divinity. Fundamentalists have no understanding of an artist. As they see it, the Creator saw it all at once, did it perfectly (in a week), and brought it out. Lo and behold, it's been perfect ever since. He never failed once. We're the patsies. We ruined it by not keeping our noses clean enough to breathe in all of God's laws and directions. But according to them, God's design was perfect from the start. The Fundamentalists are charging full speed into a profound contradiction of themselves.

Here is what I understand to be the position of present-day Intelligent Design. It would say: We don't know exactly which processes of

*natural selection, mutation, and evolution are directly related to the
Intelligence used to create the world, but we are saying that what
does exist out there in nature bespeaks the presence of an Intelligence
behind it at some level—maybe at some removes back. But it is certainly opposed to those Fundamentalists who would say God created
the world in one instant six thousand years ago. Intelligent Design
people do say that evolution cannot explain all the appearance of design that we see in natural life. Intelligence had also to be involved.*

It certainly makes great sense to me that Intelligent Design is one of the elements in evolution. What I find comfortable, even agreeable about it as a notion, is that if we do have
a God who created a universe as manifold as ours, how indeed
could it have been done without Intelligent Design, without
having notions that this is where to go here, this is how to
change that now? The other element present, which I must
emphasize over and over, is that if God is not All-Powerful,
His creations went out into an existence that didn't necessarily receive them with generosity. In many circumstances, God
might well have had to say to Himself or Herself, "I didn't
anticipate this."

Tectonic plates—

Exactly. How much simpler to assume God didn't expect
that disaster. He was aghast.

*Or, to engage the argument, the tectonic plates are just another ex-
ample of the randomness and the chaos of the universe.*

But the Artist works to extract order from chaos. I would
not even say that chaos is a lack of order. Chaos is a mix of

sets that are too complex and too disparate to be ordered within the onlooker's consciousness. If you will, each element in chaos can have its own set of laws and processes, but that organization comes into conflict with another set of orders, and they are incompatible. They erode each other when they do not tear each other apart. I also would postulate Malign Design. By which I would posit forces not at all congenial to God's concepts of creativity. How do I arrive at this? Because nowhere in existence do you find a free ride. Anything that comes along that seems wonderful in the beginning meets opposition, encounters enjambments. Sooner or later, a forward motion is stunned, hindered, or stopped.

Do you then espouse a theory of Intelligent Design that has imperfect design?

The new design can be excellent until it runs into chaotic elements that could not be anticipated.

That's imperfection.

"Perfection" may not be the word to use here. Sometimes you see creatures in the universe who are so exquisitely designed that the moment one speaks of Intelligent Design, you say, Of course! Orchids, snowflakes, panthers. Evolution, by trial and error, could not have produced some of the more beautiful forms we see in the animal world. Racehorses. Certain dogs. Even if we find most insect forms repellent, nonetheless, when we look at them under magnification, we can see the extraordinary work that went into their development. It becomes harder to believe that evolution said, "Yes, the six joints on this particular leg will have curves as wonderful as scimitars because this is the only way this species can survive." It is easier to believe that the limb was designed for beauty as well as for function.

You know the cliché: You put a million monkeys in a room with a million typewriters—eventually one of them will produce War and Peace *or* Hamlet.

Go to a computer for that. The number is too vast to be interesting.

Let me give you another refutation of Intelligent Design—

I'm listening.

In the vastness of the universe, there are billions of stars and solar systems and galaxies. By our limited knowledge, of the ones we've looked at, not one comes close to having the basics to design a universe—that is, the water and rain, the flora and fauna that went into creating our amazing, complex organic system. There's nothing like that anywhere else that we can see in the universe. Couldn't it be we're just a fluke of the cosmos? In so vast a universe, with so many possibilities, finally there is one planet that developed out of the equivalent of megabillions of monkeys pounding out Hamlet.

But I would call that an argument *for* Intelligent Design. Because we find nothing elsewhere that works like anything on earth—all the fineness of detail we have here—I see that precisely as a powerful argument for Intelligent Design.

What, then, is the function of all the other stars and galaxies?

All we can say with any authority is that in our solar system, the earth seems to be the only planet that is now alive with creatures. So it may be that other gods—conceivably gods more powerful than ours—have had large failures. It is possible that the earth succeeded in accomplishing something other planets were unable to exercise. Given the limited powers of astronomy today, there seem to be no near galaxies that are comparable. But there may be. There are so many possibilities. All we can begin to say is that it seems reasonable to posit a god for our universe.

For our solar system.

For our solar system. It may be that this God failed with other planets, prior to the earth. I won't even begin to approach that. I will repeat that it is far more difficult to comprehend the complexity of our existence if God does not exist—because then we are back to the monkeys writing *Hamlet,* and that is hard to believe. It is much easier to suppose that *Hamlet* is a part of human design. And if it's not—if it did take trillions of monkeys to produce the equivalent—what a waste. There has to be the assumption, along with everything else, that existence is moving toward a goal and therefore lives within the boundaries of an economy. It is also possible that existence itself, in the deepest, most cosmic sense, is in peril. Of necessity, therefore, it is moving forward. It is as if we will have a rendezvous with extinction if we do not reach a certain period or place by a given time, as if indefinables have to be achieved in order to protect the continuation of this existence.

This is what I would term reasonable paranoia, by which I mean that one can try to think about it without diving into dire declines or flaming into manic outbursts. But if there is some footing to this last assumption, then Intelligent Design is a crucial part of it.

Fine. I want to take a chance with our discussion. You tell us that if you think at all like a philosopher, it is because you have been a novelist all your life. Splendid! I want to see what you can do with a parallel that's apparent to me. Novelists, after all, create worlds.

We do try to. Some of us. Sometimes.

Good. Let's take the notion of Intelligent Design in relation to the novel.

Well, as I did say before, true artisans like Henry James and Hemingway gave themselves over entirely to design. It's as if their works were put together to live entirely by themselves. Perhaps, as creators, they felt less need to look for support in the breath and raw facts of existence.

All right. Let me take another leap. Is there any relation between your assumption that Intelligent Design is confronted and altered by existence and your disdain for plot in your novels?

That's a good question. But before I get into it, let me say a word or two about James Joyce. Unlike Hemingway and Henry James—who are not only great novelists and avatars of Intelligent Design so pure that their works, once designed and fashioned, tend to live by themselves—Joyce, to the contrary, plays at the very edge of chaos, which is why it is very hard to get near to Joyce. A common reflex is to look to avoid all that. But Joyce did undertake to organize whole areas of chaos.

I don't want to lose my point. In many essays, many interviews, you have said, in effect, "I don't worry about plot. Plot is much less important to me than character." You always have a storyline, but your plots are not—

They're not clockwork.

No. So I've wondered if for you to have a plot that is neat and tight and ordered would run counter to your ideas of metaphysics.

Good. Plot, if you will, is Intelligent Design. It is interesting to me—and I thought about it a lot in the years I wrote *Harlot's Ghost* because the CIA is a perfect example of plot—that is, Intelligent Design—coming into contact and conflict with the world. The reason I don't like plots to prevail is that they don't allow the figures in the book, the characters, to push their own limits to the point where they make the plot unacceptable and so throw the design into chaos.

Borges offers brilliant models to underline this risk. Borges wrote five- and six-page short stories that start with incredible plots. Then the plots get shattered. All in five or six pages. Incredible stories. He, like Joyce, was fascinated with making attacks on the nature of chaos. Borges showed us for all time—talk about a novelist's novelist! He said to us: "Look at what you're all doing. You take yourselves too seriously. You miss the fact that once a plot is shattered, life still goes on. Another species of life begins and you have to deal with it."

Take this back to Intelligent Design. God looks for Intelligent Design. Then new Intelligent Design gets itself worked upon by existence. The Wright brothers designed an airplane. Don't we know that! And after they got it up in the air for the first time, and it flew a few hundred feet, they went back to the drawing board to refine the knowledge received. Intelligent Design cannot exist without experience. So long as it remains Intelligent Design, pure but untested, it remains analogous to any number of very talented young novelists who don't publish because they never get their book to the point where they want it to be seen. They will not put their book out on the waters. Whereas God, I will obviously argue, tends to launch each Intelligent Design to see what happens to it. That is how God learns, how He proceeds to the next Intelligent Design.

Let me enjoy one extreme aspect of this notion. In my book about Henry Miller, I spoke of three men coming into a hostess's living room: Henry James, Hemingway, and Henry Miller. Each takes off his hat, and behold! To their vast surprise—they had no prior knowledge of this—a cow turd is steaming under each hat. I then go on to say Henry James might have perished from so awful an experience. Hemingway would have gone into a depression—he would have seen it as emblematic of the nature of life: Just when life seemed something you could enjoy, unexpected disasters shattered your mood. And Miller would have said, "Good Lord, how did that turd get on my head? And just look at the hostess. Her nostrils are quivering, or is that because of her twat? She is so excited—what a wonderful moment!" Miller is an example of someone who couldn't stay with a plot for five minutes because he wanted to run right into the world and discover something new about himself and/or the world. He is at one extreme, Henry James at the other. Between them lies the effective use of Intelligent Design.

But what would Joyce have done?

Joyce is so much of a genius, I won't try to trim his coat-tails. I don't know what he would have done with the cow turd.

I think he would have appreciated it.

He might have looked for a conflation of the twenty-two words in fifteen languages that illumine the concept of shit. What would be the wonderful sound he would come up with? On the other hand, he could have felt removed from the situation. It was not life he was interested in so much as language.

I disagree. The first person to wipe his ass in a novel is Leopold Bloom.

Your point. . . .

You recently criticized Sartre's existentialism for being floorless, without floor.

Without a foundation.

Because, as you put it, "It is, after all, near to impossible for a philosopher to explore how we are here without entertaining some notion of what the prior force might have been." Therefore, if we grant your limited God as that prior force, then I'm compelled to ask what force preceded your God? I assume you would choose infinite regress rather than a Prime Mover?

Again, I refuse to be blindsided by such questions. There's a story you're probably familiar with, of Bertrand Russell and an old lady—Russell is talking about the origin of the universe and how it is not knowable. An old lady in the audience speaks up. She says, "On the contrary, Professor Russell. I know the basis of the universe." He says, "What is it, Madam?" She replies, "The universe is resting upon a turtle." "Madam, that's very helpful, but what is the turtle resting on?" And she replies, "It's turtles all the way down!"

I do remember that.

I'm not going to get trapped in arguments that ask me to explain what came behind the God I'm talking about.

But you beat Sartre over the head because he won't allow for a force behind humanity. Why can't we then try to find out . . . I'm not looking to refute you, but—

Let me put it this way: We first have to become close to God and helpful to God—large questions we haven't even entered. God is not only an element in existence but a moral presence. Until we can feel we are some kind of great help to God, why should God trust us? You remember, at the end of *Harlot's Ghost*, Hugh Montague goes off on this—to me—

intriguing speech that God, having decided that the advent of humans was not yet to be trusted, proceeded to then create the illusion of evolution. In reality—so goes Harlot's thesis—the earth was created entire, ex nihilo, by God in six days. He then laid in evidence all over the earth and in the seas that evolution had done it instead over millions of years. Implied in all that is a suggestion that until we get close enough to God to feel we are in some kind of alliance, can we begin to have some knowledge of what might be behind God? But that won't happen until we get nearer. Sartre doesn't let us point in that direction at all.

You do see moral relations between God and humans as a possibility, however?

Ultimately. If things go better than I expect they will.

I don't know if you're familiar with the philosopher David Hume—

Yes, in college. I had him. Vaguely, you might say.

Well, Hume got into the argument for Intelligent Design. One of the proofs of St. Thomas Aquinas for the existence of God is indeed the argument from design. It goes back that far, hundreds of years. Aquinas has many proofs of God's existence, but the fifth one was that design is so perfect in the universe—he didn't even see beyond the solar system—

Right there, you run smack into the most obdurate aspect of Catholicism, the insistence of Catholicism on God's perfection. What characterizes my idea of Intelligent Design is that it is partial—not perfect, but partial—a partial improvement. I'm glad I have the novel to fall back upon as a metaphor for this. When I write a novel, it's an attempt to come up with a piece of intelligent design, but it's never perfect. Some parts are better than others. If it goes into publication, the critical returns come back. Very often, those returns have little relation to what you wrote. Occasionally, they do. Slowly, over the years, you learn more. By the end of your life, you may be wiser as a novelist than when you started. The heart of one of my notions, then, is that God, too, is always looking to become wiser. What you create may, in the beginning, not be understood all too well or, for that matter, not be fashioned well enough yet.

Listen to this collision between Aquinas and David Hume: Hume criticized the argument from design. In particular, he emphasized there is no legitimate way to infer the properties of God from the qualities of the world, His creation. For instance, Hume questioned, how can we be sure the world was not created by a team? Or, this may be but only one of many attempts at Creation, the first few having been botched. Or, on the other hand, our world could be the puerile first attempt of an infant deity who afterward abandoned it, ashamed of his lame performance.

That last doesn't fulfill my notion of the passion implicit in the artistry of God. I can't conceive of a great artist ever junking a work and just moving on—not if that has been his major opus. I certainly do lean to the notion that our world is God's major opus. But Hume did put it well on the argument for a perfect universe. From my point of view, he was correct in seeing that as near to intolerable. The notion of a perfect universe scrambles people's brains.

All the same, the Catholic Church is a fabulously successful institution—and probably because of that insistence on a perfect universe.

Fabulously successful, yes, but you could also say the Jewish religion has been fabulously successful in one way—the Jews didn't perish. But what a price they paid! And, I'd add, what a price Catholics have paid. To have created a Church that brought so much architectural beauty to the world, so much musical beauty, so much ritual beauty—and then to be locked into a set of notions they can't let go of, that explain nothing, but that elevate contradictions and magnify spiritual and moral confusion.

You know, when they are beautiful, the services of organized religion move me. I feel, "How tragic. How painful." All this devotion, all this loyalty, and it goes into an intellectual sump. It explains nothing. All you are finally asked to believe is that God will be there to hear your prayers, God will welcome us when we die—as if that's all God has to do.

What about Hume's idea that the universe might have been created by a team?

Not impossible. Not impossible. It explains one of my basic notions. The team soon fell out of sorts with one another, and we ended up with God and the Devil.

A joint endeavor—

Like those South Seas Companies in the 1700s.

If, as you say, the Creator is an Artist and not all creative works are equally successful, wouldn't this lead quite easily to racism? That is, couldn't the "inferior race," however it's defined, whether the non-Aryans scapegoated by the Nazis or the "ice people" of the Afrocentric extremists, simply be one of God's less successful creations?

Well, I reject the language of the question. One of the absolute disasters that Hitler brought to human understanding was an abuse of the concept of race. Because race offers us great clues. It is perfectly possible—and here again, one can only speculate—but it is perfectly possible that races, in the beginning, were Intelligent Designs for different situations. In other words, for people in the tropics, God was saying, "Well, how can I design the heating system of their bodies so they can bear the excessive warmth more easily?" And He made separate adjustments for the north. We're discovering that living in separate climates produces different relaxations and strictures of the throat. Languages reflect that. Mind you, God as the Artist might be discovering within the material itself where the continuation might be. Certain sculptors talk about how they do not know exactly what the work will become until they cut into the marble. It is the marble that discloses what they must do with the next stroke. The same process of discovery may be present in human or animal design. The environment plays a mighty role.

*Your conception of God as Artist assumes that God is both vastly—
but not all—good and vastly—but not all—powerful. But why
couldn't God be not very compassionate but instead immensely curi-
ous? He could be fascinated by, but not especially compassionate
toward, Creation, much like a child who winds up toys and watches
them slam into each other and chortles at the smashup. You say, "In
other words, why are there volcanoes? Because God was not a perfect
engineer." Or because, like a two-year-old, God found the noise and
fury fascinating and amusing—maybe even the shrieks of the dying
fascinating and amusing. To use the ultimately reductive phrase, you
keep assuming God is a nice person. That seems a bit arbitrary.*

It is arbitrary, and it could be my conditioning. I grew up
in a household that was as religious as the next—it wasn't a
dogma-driven atmosphere, but I do remember my mother on
Friday night praying before a lit candelabrum, praying to the
Shekhina, a Hebrew word for the wife of God, and there
were tears in my mother's eyes. A feeling of great tenderness
came from her. I think I always took it for granted that God
was compassionate in relation to us.

Now, the arguments you just raised cannot be refuted. How
can I declare, "No, God is not going in for capers." Of course,
God could engage in mean acts. But to me, the notion that God
and the Devil are in conflict with each other makes more sense.
So I believe we've got this one God who is more good than not.

Well, your mother's father was a rabbi.

Yes. He studied to be a rabbi in Lithuania, but by the time
he came over here, the only way he could make his living was

as a peddler. Then he moved to a town in New Jersey called
Long Branch, where he opened a shop and worked as a
butcher. There was only one synagogue in Long Branch, so
when the regular rabbi was ill or off on vacation, my grandfather stood in for him. And my mother was proud of this. The
fundamental snobbery of the Jews—it was much better to be
a rabbi than a butcher. As a contrarian Jew, I was delighted; it
gave me two different strains to develop.

*Well, I'm thinking of your mother's devotion and the tear in her
eye—obviously, she must have come from a pretty religious household.*

My grandfather was most religious—he began studying
the Talmud when he was four years old. One of the best
things to be said about the Talmud is that it's very hard to become a Fundamentalist while studying it. It's too easy if you
live only with the Torah but difficult when reading the Talmud. Unlike the Torah (which is the first five books of the
Old Testament), the Talmud inquires into the nuances of
things. For instance, in that long-gone age, people brought
animals to the temple to be sacrificed. Very often there were
small disasters—a poor man might have decided to sacrifice
his prize heifer because his child was fearfully ill. But on his
entrance into the temple, the heifer would defecate. Well,
the Talmud is ready to focus on just where it defecated. Was
it outside on the patio? Or did it do the job on the steps? In
the vestibule? In the aisle? At the altar approach? Did it defecate on the altar? Outrageous! For all these are separate vio-
lations of the most holy and so call for different penalties. In

certain cases, the animal can still be sacrificed. At other sites, like the altar, the animal is lost completely. It cannot be eaten. In the Talmud, there are, nonetheless, all these efforts to find zones of relative compatibility between God's laws and human needs—so the Talmud becomes the opposite of the Old Testament (and needless to say, the New Testament), where the law is, in effect, inflexible.

Well, there is a certain measure of Orphic ambiguity in the utterances of Christ.

I wouldn't call it ambiguity. I see it as the wars of committees that are looking to fix what His behavior might have been—for their theological purposes, not his. So occasionally they were at odds. But each side of the disagreement was inflexible.

Did your mother talk much about her father?

She adored him, and he was a very kind man. One story I loved when I was a kid: She once said, "My mother worked so hard in the butcher shop, and we as children worked hard, too. We'd get angry at my father because whenever a poor woman would come in and he'd weigh the meat she bought, he'd put his finger under the scale so it cost her less. And we thought, That's all very well, but money is being taken away from us."

He was obviously a compassionate man.

I was only four when he died. But I like to think so.

VIII

On Theodicy

MICHAEL LENNON: *Any venture that looks to deal with the philosophical problem of evil fits this category. And there are many. I will cite a number of theodicies, but there are so many I will move to the next so soon as you, from your point of view, have done your best to refute the premise.*

NORMAN MAILER: Agreed.

God's ultimate purpose, some philosophers say, is to glorify Himself. He, by definition He alone, is infinitely entitled to do that without vanity. But He does allow evil to exist so we will appreciate His goodness all the more. It is analogous to the way that the blind man healed by Jesus appreciated sight more than those around him who had never experienced such a condition.

Let me take up first what I have never understood. Why is there this enormous desire in God to be glorified? Why is that so acceptable to so many branches of religion? We laugh at people who insist on being constantly glorified. We speak of neurotic movie stars or spoiled athletes, crazy generals and impossible authors, mad kings and greed-bag tycoons. One of the few things we all seem to agree on is that excessive vanity, once it has grown into a thing in itself, is dire. By that logic, a God-sized vanity is hard to comprehend. Where is the need for it?

Maybe we can change "glorified" to "loved." God wants to be loved.

Why does God need to be loved? That's a large question. It may be true, but if God needs to be loved, then I think we are entitled to start posing a few questions. Is God's need to be loved so crucial because God, like us, is overextended? When, after all, do we have our greatest need to be appreciated? It is precisely when we are worn thin—precisely those times when our courage, our stamina, our determination, our belief that we possess worth are attenuated. At such times, we are more in need of love.

Are you saying that is where God is now?

It is the only justification I can comprehend for God needing so much adoration from us.

Moving to my second point, do you have any interest in the argument that He allows evil to exist in order to intensify our love for Him all the more?

I find that strange. I've always been bothered by the excessive love that God appears to demand—or, worse, that the churchmen who rule His places of worship insist upon. "Jesus needs your love, Jesus wants your love." Well, Jesus is giving love, presumably. Does He need it in order to return it? What they're saying—without understanding, because they never follow anything to conclusion—but one of the elements in their thinking that repels most serious young people away from theology is that Fundamentalists, for example, seem to make a point of *not* contemplating the consequences of their thought. For if God does need a great deal of love, then why? Why? The question has to be asked. Doesn't it suggest that we dwell in a situation where God's fate depends upon our development as well—the good or evil world that we are developing?

Now, all we have to work with in these theological speculations is what we know from our own experiences. People who need love desperately are not often in good shape. If God created us in His or Her image, which I do believe, then God must also want us to understand some real portion of what is going on in His universe. It is to God's advantage, I would argue, for us to understand what God's desires might be. Unless, on the other hand, human history has been so vile and so awful, so permeated by the large and little triumphs of the Devil, that God has a legitimate fear of being betrayed by mankind so soon as humans obtain enough power. If that is so, exorbitant requests for love become even more disturbing.

Here is another theodicy: Evil is one of the means by which God can test humanity and see if we are worthy of His grace and His love. The evil and the suffering that come to us prove to be educational; they can make us better people. He is testing us, and the tests are good for us.

I find this offensive. Apply it to a parent and a child. We test the child—and in some situations we do test a child—but do we do it to see if the child deserves our love? Literature is rife with portraits of fathers and mothers of that detestable ilk.

Consider the second part: It is educational for the parents. It makes us better people. We do that with children—we do test them to improve them. We say, "Now that you've been through this, you're a better person for it." We do that all the time to our children.

On the other hand, there is also large vanity in the assumption that God knows all about evil. Why not try to live with the notion that God is trying to discover what evil is about? What if evil is, at present, more bottomless than good? Isn't that a corollary of the notion that God is not All-Powerful? What, after all, is God's relation to Evil? Is He trying to discover more about it? May it be that God doesn't comprehend Evil that well, any more than parents are always quick to understand when children are sliding toward evil. Are parents always the first to know?

It was Dostoyevsky who said suffering is the sole origin of consciousness, that only through suffering could we improve our comprehension of the world around us a little more. Do you reject that?

I can agree that suffering is, yes, a mighty educator, but it is also an immensely expensive one. Some learn a great deal from it; all too many are reduced if not destroyed. Suffering can maim more spirit than it creates. Some learn best by suffering through small stages that enable one to shift one's uglier habits.

A form of suffering.

A modest form. If I want something, and I can't have it, I may be suffering like a child. Whereas Dostoyevsky was referring to suffering at a level so intense that one had to wonder whether one could go on. Was existence worthwhile? Suffering of that order can become too intense. Some people turn to suicide. And it can be true that a number do pass through such storms of the soul and return not emotionally crippled—indeed, have much to offer. But most have lost too much.

Let me offer another theodicy, the "now and then." Evil and pain exist in this world, but only as a prelude to the afterlife. There, no pain will exist. So God offers a balance: much suffering, pain, and evil in this world, but in the other there will be none. The scales balance.

That is comparable to a man thinking, "I'm poor, but there will come a day when I am wealthy." Of course, the poor man has nothing to offer concerning the way and the means by which he will become wealthy. He has nothing but his hankering. By the same token, any notion that we will live in peace and beauty afterward may be naught but our need for future promises. Are we looking for salesmanship? "You won't know what true happiness is until you buy this wonderful car. You'll thank me for having sold it to you."

In the theodicies you've presented so far, there is always the assumption that God is in control of our fates from beginning to end. By my lights, theological misdirection rears up right at the commencement of the thesis. Anyone who looks even casually at the variety of incredible animals who have come down through evolution (and/or Intelligent Design) has to assume that God may have said to Himself at a certain point, "This little animal, this macaw, is going to be the best of its species." Then, it turned out that it wasn't. So God moved on and made a better bird or made a better hedgehog or a better pig. Then, man came into it and began in his turn to alter the animals—and often, improve them (as we see every year on TV at the American Kennel Club). Yet at the moment you accept a darker notion of existence—that is, live with the assumption that there are hazards and perils added by the Devil, then God's effort becomes a contest where no one, human or divine, necessarily knows which side may win. Many might be ready to commit themselves to God in such a contest. But for contrast, look at how our sense of challenge is reduced if this is all happening to illuminate God's greater glory. All we have to do is remain patient and pass through our suffering— because a happy ending is guaranteed. No! I much prefer the assumption of the Greeks that tragedy lies next to happiness, and both compose the staples of our existence. We can live with the hope that it may all turn out well, but such hope will be empty unless we are also prepared to live with a tragic outcome. We need to have the bravery to proceed, but in no way are we entitled to proclaim that a wonderful heaven is waiting for all of us, and we need only keep our minds clean and, most preferably, theologically inert.

The fourth theodicy is one of Maya. Illusion. This is how some deal with the question of Evil. They say: What humans consider to be evil or suffering is either an illusion or it's unimportant. Events that are thought to be evil, such as death by natural disaster, are really not so. It could all be part of God's scheme. Eastern thought— Taoism, Buddhism, Hinduism—takes this stance. They do not engage the problem of evil. You are mistaken, they would claim, if you think it is really there.

This argument could survive into the twentieth century. Then, the Holocaust shattered it. Shattered it *force majeure.* The particular facts were so odious that they dictated the need for a different approach.

Contemplate also gulags and the atom bomb. Excessive human suffering was intensified by at least one order of magnitude. In consequence, the notion that evil is illusion grows offensive. Of course, Maya assumes that all of the "outside world"—good, evil, and neutral—is illusion, wonderful, lovely outer events are as illusory as suffering. It's all Maya. But to repeat, I find that odious. I suggest that we at our maximum are more than the equal of any holy cow in any Hindu pasture. Indeed, the notion that all life is illusion is comforting to the ethos of the upper classes of India. They can salve their bad conscience at the sight of the hideous poverty around them. It's all illusion, they can tell themselves happily and most conveniently.

If you believe in karma, as I do—believe not only in rebirth but in subtle divine judgment (hopefully it is subtle)
concerning the manner in which you will be reborn—another
part of me remains sardonic and expects that God may have
His or Her occasional problem operating the mechanics of
reincarnation. If populations die at a steady rate with only a
statistical spike here and there—a local earthquake, a terrible
storm, a flood—God can receive and judge incoming souls.
Forgive so crude a presentation of celestial mechanics, but it
must serve for the moment. When reincarnation is flooded
with a huge number of deaths that have no meaning—
because they are abrupt, even near instantaneous, without
warning, and provide no opportunity to die with grace and so
leave the victims bereft of awareness at the moment of their
death—obliged to die marooned altogether from any sense of
why they now must die—then they enter reincarnation with
less preparation within. The most sensitive mortal anticipa-
tions may have been lopped off. It is worth repeating. I would
argue that a sudden, unexpected death is much worse than
death that comes to one after a modicum of thought and fear
and resolve and expectation. I believe there is a difference,
and it may be profound.

So I think the Holocaust ravaged many human entrances
into death. Reincarnation was flooded with near-to-nameless
dead.

*Was it so different from trench warfare in the First World War,
where they were killing 150,000 people in a week? Surely, that*

equals the rate of people being exterminated in the Holocaust. By the time the First World War was over, something like thirty million people were gone.

I believe it's analogous but not identical. The deaths were, after all, taking place on both sides.

So every time this has happened, like at the Battle of Stalingrad, all of those—

When you go into a battle like Stalingrad, you are, at least, aware that you may die. What was diabolical about the Nazi camps is that they were most careful not to prepare people for death. It is worth repeating: They did not state, "We are going to gas you today." On the contrary, they told the concentration-camp inmates that since they were lice ridden and filthy, they would receive showers, courtesy of the camp. So be so good as to undress. Those prisoners who were most obsessed with cleanliness trooped happily into the gas chambers. A minute later, they were dying with fire in their lungs and screaming, "You lied, you cheated me." I am arguing that for a thousand people to die in a large room while experiencing one hideous instant of betrayal is to feel that God has betrayed them.

In contrast, the soldiers in Stalingrad knew there was a large chance they were going to perish. That, I would submit, offered less grievous problems to the powers of reincarnation than the gassings of the Holocaust. I repeat: It is so important to have a sense of why you are dying. I go so far as to believe that that can prepare you for your next existence.

Are you saying God was not able to accommodate many who were
ready for reincarnation?

What is basic in the universe? Certainly the laws concerning the conservation of energy—we know that you cannot do
everything at once for everyone. All existence seems to be
built on that set of proportions. So to assume that God is in
complete command of reincarnation is equal to assuming that
He or She never suffers even a passing despair before huge,
unforeseen disasters and their concomitant depletions of divine energy. Indeed, why must we assume that God antici-
pates every event? Or is in command of every energy for
every occasion? He or She created our world, but that
doesn't mean every oncoming situation was delineated in advance. Hardly so. History, because of the ongoing actions of
God and the Devil, is not always open to prediction, not even
to them. Before the future of history even divinities take
pause. Neither side commands all the contemplations.

What happened, then, to those victims of the gas chambers?

I would offer this speculation. I would say most of those
who desired reincarnation did receive it, but in unsatisfactory
fashion. This would derive from the argument I proposed
earlier that the closest we come to Heaven or Hell is to encounter some angelic witty presence who decides how you
are going to be reincarnated and where. When God's wit is
present, that is as close as you will get to Heaven or Hell, either the knowledge that you will have a better life or a poorer
one at the start of your next life. But when the Creator is not

functioning at His or Her best but is too beleaguered, too extenuated, too despairing, too exhausted, then the choices made for reincarnation can be deemed gross—there's not enough of God to go around. It is a way of saying the Holocaust deadened God's wit. Too much was happening at once. God, I will repeat once more, is not inexhaustible.

I hear what you say, but why is it more difficult for God to assign a new birth to someone who died in the Holocaust than someone who died in the trenches? I don't see the difference.

Okay, let's put it this way—you have been a teacher. You certainly won't dispute the suggestion that you can walk into certain classrooms and see that certain students are ready to learn, whereas others look lethargic. Some are eager to be in class, and others are there because it is compulsory. So I am saying that when you die with great bitterness in your heart, you are harder to reach. How does this not apply to reincarnation? I am now improvising outrageously, but allow me. Let us say that the Monitoring Angel comes by, takes one quick look, and has a sense of how the recently expired soul before him can prove strong here, weak there, and might well deserve to go to this rebirth or that. In normal situations, he can make quick decisions. But if the dead person's soul is in disarray, then it can be analogous to you deciding how to give necessary counsel to a student who has come into your room in fearful drugged-up condition. You don't necessarily know whether they should be assigned to a given class. I think this can carry over to what I'm talking about.

Next one. The big picture, the fifth theodicy. God's divine plan is good. What we see as evil is not really evil. Rather, it is part of a divine design that actually is good. Our limitations prevent us from seeing the larger picture. Certainly you'll grant that God envisions more than we do.

Certainly.

So things we think are a terrible tragedy turn out a year later to be positive experiences.

Yes, the army: the worst experience of my life, and the most valuable. That's one thing. But to build a theological system on this theodicy may be excessively hopeful. It does not explain evil at all. It does not justify the Holocaust. The first person who can show me how the Holocaust was good for God's purposes will alter my thinking drastically.

The great example is Judas. Judas was a traitor, a betrayer, yet he was absolutely necessary to God's plan—

How do you know what God's plan was? You're taking the received wisdom of theologians who have been living with these enigmas for two thousand years and coming up with the answers that serve their respective needs. But what they conclude may have nothing to do with cosmic or earthly reality. In *The Gospel According to the Son*, I concluded that two things happened because of the crucifixion. God lost to the Devil and, worse, he had expected to win. He thought Jesus was going to change humankind profoundly and immediately. He did not foresee the end. God, having so much to oversee all at once, is not necessarily focused on what each one of His particular Creations is capable of. While I'm willing to assume that Jesus was His bold stroke, I would add that in chess when a really bold move is made and the player is not sure how it is going to turn out, you record it with an exclamation point plus a question mark. I would say God's expectation for Jesus was both an exclamation point and a question mark. Then, like many another bold move, it did not turn out as expected. The Devil won—Jesus was tortured. At this point, God in His brilliance came up with an answer to the Devil. He gave us to believe that His son actually died for our sins. What a human chord was struck! But to suggest that this was all planned in advance—crucifixion and resurrection—dubious. God may well have been responding to a crushing defeat with claims of half a victory. That makes more sense to me: God was rewriting the depths of what had happened after the events ensued—which is exactly what humans do all the time. We call it history. It is one of our fundamental activities. I suppose I even offer the assumption that not only is God like us in many ways but, indeed, He or She also has an ego to protect, that is, a necessary reservoir of confidence sufficient to keep striving.

The next theodicy argues that evil is not the cause but the consequence of people failing to observe God's will. Universal, reciprocated love would solve most of the problems that lead to the evils in the world.

Well, let me go back to something I said earlier. God is searching for a deeper set of meanings in evil. Conceivably, God may feel that He does not understand evil all that satisfactorily. Evil has aspects that God's understanding may not penetrate. My repetitive notion is that God, like us, seeks to learn. Maybe at the commencement, whatever form it really took, some vast deity, very far removed, said, "All right, new and most youthful deity, this will be your territory. Do what You can with it. If You can."

That's a Gnostic idea.

"And if You fail—well, it's happened to other deities. All the same, You are an artist, the best artist we have available just now for Your assigned part of the cosmos." Given this scenario, our young God soon discovers that He or She has a great deal to learn about evil—and is soon fascinated with it.

Well, you have a view of evil as a powerful, dynamic force.

Yes, at the least I see evil as looking to destroy the part of the universe that we know—our world.

Emerson said there really is no evil, just the absence of good, but that there are degrees of good.

Too easy. It enables us to go to sleep at night without pang or fear. But on the nights when one can't sleep, sometimes you can feel there's evil in the room, evil in your heart, evil in people around you—not all the time, but (rarely—thank God!) on those occasions when one's felt such a presence, you certainly cannot say that it is not really evil, merely a lesser degree of good. Maybe Emerson never felt an incubus on his chest. He was, after all, such a fine spirit.

Another argument: Evil is the consequence of God permitting hu-
mans to have free will. Human cruelty is the price of freedom. God
gave us this freedom, and He cannot interfere. Without the possi-
bility to choose to do good or evil, humanity would be robots.

That's the best, single, strongest argument. But theologians wriggle out of it. They put God back in control by the
end of the philosophical day.

Well, yes, at the end of time, God does take over again. This is a
testing time.

Here is exactly where existentialism needs to rear up. Yes,
God had to give us free will in order to find out about us. He
could learn so much more about us provided we were given
free will. But, of necessity, the door had to be left open to the
Devil. This was a move done, perhaps—on a cosmic level—in
fear and trembling. Yes, great fear because the final answer
had to be left open. It was not free will unless the Devil had
something like an equal opportunity to influence humans.

I would add that by now it is a tripartite war. If it is only
a contest between God and the Devil, and we are no more
than the field on which it all takes place—some species of
Astroturf—then we still do not have free will. We have to be
equal as players to God and the Devil. That has to open a new
kind of fear for us. It could all go down to disaster. The usual
supposition, however, is that God will finally be victorious,
and, yes, we, His soldiers, will all go to Heaven, a view held
for centuries—no longer, however, I would say. Now it is as
if any one of these three forces can triumph. Many will now

even conceive of a universe without God and the Devil. I don't pretend to know how to speculate on this. Let's say it is not inconceivable that man may become more powerful in relation to God and the Devil. If They have exhausted each other, we may even arrive at a point where it does become man and woman's world, our humans' world.

What would make that come about?

Technology. It's obvious—well, obvious to me—that every effort is being made in these years to replicate a human being and, once done, forge armies of them. It might take two centuries, but it does seem to be what we humans are hell-bent on doing. At that point, free will will have grown so large and so livid that it will be looking to replace God. I naturally see that as absolutely disastrous. If I have been ready to question God's judgment on many a matter, I am wholly reluctant to put faith in our judgment. We are far from equipped to deal with the cosmos.

Here is the last theodicy. The eighth. God is a righteous judge. And so people get what they deserve. If someone suffers, it is because they have committed a sin that merits such suffering.

What if a divine balance has been disrupted? We had a different relation to existence ten thousand years ago. You had to hunt an animal down if you wished to eat meat. Now the beasts are brought to stockyards. Flesh for consumption is slaughtered in disagreeable fashion. Sows are kept in cribs so small they do not have room to move once they are fattened. The world of nature once lived on the basis that nearly everything contributed to the feeding chain. Add reincarnation, and the cycles of life and death were taken care of. This was the original conception. Today, as one example, contemporary agribusiness has skewed it. So, in like fashion, can we speak of the earlier human notion that excessive evil was compensated for? The idea that if you were killed before your time, reincarnation could make adjustments may no longer be operative. Yet it still remains the only explanation I know for why many young soldiers are, when tested, ready to die in battle. I think they have a sense—comparable in some degree to the terrorists who are blowing themselves up—that they are going somewhere special. Right or wrong, this is their belief. It is a deep belief—indeed, so profound that one cannot necessarily ignore the possibility that it is real. But repeat this theodicy, would you?

God is righteous. People get what they deserve.

God does the best He or She can do. That doesn't mean people get what they deserve. If they did, the universe would be equal to a clock.

Would you agree that it was inevitable once God gave us free will and intelligence that technology would follow?

No. I am working against the tide on this one, but it could be that at a certain point God hoped and expected all of us would become psychic. Great entertainers would be so intense in their art that men and women all over the world could experience the performance. Of course, it did not happen. We looked instead for technological means of communicating. And that blunted the possibility of such fine senses. It helps to account in part for the near-mute, somewhat odd and wistful sense we acquire when we watch a world event on television.

I would say that if you put people in a physical world, they are going to invent the wheel. And once they do, technology follows from that.

No, sir. No, sir. Electronics has nothing to do with the wheel.

So when we went from a mechanical universe to an electronic universe—

A leap not anticipated. Or such is my supposition.

Now, most people who believe in reincarnation do expect that sooner or later they will reach enlightenment or some equitable resting place and look back upon the problems and sufferings of earthly life as no more than way stations on the journey. But I can't agree. I think reincarnation makes no sense if the end is foretold. I can't emphasize this enough. None of my arguments makes sense if the end is known. I think it is precisely because the end is unknown that human terror sits at the root of every theology, as it has for millennia. It is so difficult for humans to accept the likelihood that this world is as open and undecipherable, as chaotic, as wayward, as playful, as perverse, as unexpected as, in secret, we fear it is. I think this is what has driven any number of theologians to the notion that it has all been foretold, that the end has been granted to us. Such conclusions are not only philosophically untethered, even outrageous, but have gotten us into all sorts of trouble because a foreordained end narrows our lives, shrinks our thinking, and tends to bring out the worst in us. We become addicted to quick judgment concerning others, even as we cling to a partial optimism in which we only half believe.

In all these conversations we've had about the nature of God, your supposition has been that God makes mistakes, He is not perfect, He is much like us. But we know we have evil in us. There is evil in us as individuals and as a race. And if God is so much like us, then God does indeed have evil in Him or Her. And that explains everything—you don't need a Devil.

No, no, no, no, I don't think that's it at all. God could have a little evil in Him, and the Devil a great deal.

Let's say it's eighty-twenty. If God just has 20 percent evil, wouldn't that be enough to account for all the natural disasters and the Holocaust?

But eighty-twenty is an assumption. What if it's ninety-five–five, or ninety-eight to two?

There are theologians who take this position. They're called "open theists" and take the position that God is imperfect and has enough evil in Him—and the evil in God, coupled with the Devil, is responsible for the miseries of the world.

Well, that could certainly be an answer, and if you want to respect the Old Testament as more than a great work of literature but also as a document with some reality, you certainly have a Jehovah out there wreaking evil on a large scale as well as goodness. And it could be that God, being existential like us, was trying to reduce the amount of evil in Himself or Herself.

By doing what?

By Jehovah trying, for one thing, to get that prodigious temper under control. By daring to have a son, a great attempt to improve matters. It may be that God was always trying for more, over and over, and often deciding, "No, this move won't work." It may be that after Christ's death, He had to decide if He wished to build the Catholic Church. And maybe the Devil was joining Him. It may be easier to comprehend the history of the Catholic Church if we assume that They were building this Church together and worked in collaboration, and with some considerable unhappiness, yes, God and the Devil built it together as most unhappy and embattled partners.

In other words, God may be out on an odyssey not unrelated to ours. He or She may get better along the way but not succeed altogether.

Are you saying that many human institutions can be the creation of both God and the Devil?

Of course.

Do you see any human organizations or institutions that are free from the taint of evil? Or are they all mixed?

I think there's evil in everything.

Baseball teams . . .

You bet.

Football . . .

How not? *[pause]* One last thought. Earlier, you were advancing the argument that suffering is good for you, that submitting to God's will without complaint is virtuous. And this virtue will earn you all kinds of rewards. We will endure whatever God sends since that is our ticket to eternal bliss. Of course, if you dare to ask how a perfect God can make matters so imperfect—or, worse, unjust—the only answer you can give is, "Do not presume to understand the mind of God." Right there is the most dangerous single argument advanced by churchmen. It is exactly what drives people out of their faith because it tends to make faith brittle. Any time there is something you cannot comprehend, you are told, "It is beyond you—your faith has to carry you through this." So greater and greater spiritual loans are extracted from faith. Sooner or later, faith snaps. And people leave the Church, leave religion, cease to believe. While "Do not presume to understand the mind of God" is the most employed of the various explanations of evil, it is also, in its final effect, the most demoralizing.

I vote then, as is obvious, for an existential God who does not demand my unwavering faith but prefers instead that we look to find, despite God's flaws and ours, a core of mutual respect as we set out together to attempt to create a viable vision that can lead us into the unforeseeable future out there with its galaxies, its light-years, its enigmas, and ultimately, let us hope, its availability. Perhaps the greatest gods of the cosmos are also on a search and may not be wholly indisposed to welcome us.

IX

On Gnosticism

MICHAEL LENNON: *As we have agreed, the form of this interview will be a discussion on Gnosticism.*

NORMAN MAILER: That may be. But I have to recognize that although I have lived with that word in many a text over many a year—indeed, even gave a full reading to Elaine Pagels's *The Gnostic Gospels* some years ago—I am still not comfortable with the term. I feel ignorant of its meaning in relation to what we have talked about. One of the perils of bad memory, from which I suffer, is that one retains not nearly enough of one's serious reading. Growing old usually ensures that if you last long enough to reach your eighties, your memory will bear more resemblance to a bare wall than to a text.

*Forewarned, forewarned. I come prepared. I would start by saying
that you are hardly alone. Gnosticism is not a religious movement,
and it has been shunted pretty much off the face of the ideological
earth.*

*Here are a few of the general traits: There is, first, a disdain
for authority and Orthodoxy, which is opposed by a great belief
in studying the self. The self is regarded as a phenomenon that
you had to understand to some serious degree in order to attain
larger knowledge. In this sense, the Gnostics were close to the
Manichaeans, who were dualists but not absolute about it. Like
the Gnostics, they saw the body and the spirit as separate but mutually dependent. They were very taken with Jewish mysticism,
which of course had been present long before Christ, and so pre-
dates the Gnostics, who seem to have come into existence around
the second century B.C. and, indeed, in the beginning they were
an esoteric branch of Judaism. As you may recall from reading*
The Golden Bough, *there were many competing sects at this
time. But the Gnostics had great respect for Judaism while at the
same time valuing the Greek belief in knowledge and self-
examination.*

My knowledge of Jewish mysticism is not profound, but I
did some reading in the Kabalah and the Zohar. Neither existed, however, at that point.

*No, although later, when the Kabalah did develop, the Gnostics
were not opposed to it. They liked it. As they liked certain Buddhist
texts—*

You're talking about a thousand years later.

That's right.

The Gnostics, in other words, continue well into the Middle Ages.

Probably they end with the Inquisition.

I thought the various uprootings of the heresies in the early centuries of Christianity took care of the Gnostics. Not so?

It diminished them greatly. As I say, Gnosticism came into existence around the second century B.C. and built its ongoing strength by taking in Jewish strains, Christian strains, even Buddhist strains right up to the fourth century A.D. At that point, the Christian Church, especially under St. Irenaeus, mounted a strong campaign against them, using St. John as the point of their spear, because St. John was a great believer in Revelation, and the Gnostics were not. St. Augustine was another fierce opponent, and, of course, St. Irenaeus wrote five volumes against the heresy. Many of the tenets of Christianity—for example Original Sin, resurrection, and Jesus as the son of God—were later additions. In the year 200, however, there was no sense of Original Sin, and resurrection was barely an idea. The assumption that Jesus was God also came later. In good part, these ideas came in opposition to Gnosticism.

Could you say that the first purpose of Original Sin was to forge a powerful weapon against the Gnostics?

It seems likely. Gnosticism advocated individualism in search of enlightenment. It believed in reincarnation. It believed that all hu-

mans had some kind of divine spark. The spark may be trapped, impossible to free; one might be out of touch with it, but it was there.

I agree with so much of this.

I thought you might. It's no accident that the Fundamentalists, to the extent that they know anything about Gnosticism, see it as a disreputable part of early Christianity, best kept in the closet. If Gnosticism survives at all now, it may be among some sects who live on the border of Iraq and Iran—the Mandeans, for example, are still there. The attribute to emphasize is that in Greek, "Gnosis" means "knowledge." "Gnosticos" is someone who seeks knowledge by searching the depths of the self, looking at the self as the available ground for enlightenment. When it came to the body, they were more divided. Some saw a division between the spirit and the flesh; some felt that the flesh wasn't important at all, and therefore they could go out and fuck themselves silly because it didn't make any difference. Another branch of the Gnostics were purifiers. To the Zoroastrians, fire was holy because it purified. Water was holy. But they didn't believe in sex. Ergo, they died out. While Christianity became monolithic, Gnosticism splintered. And that is another one of the reasons it didn't survive. Nor did it have an Augustine or an Irenaeus organizing a belief system.

Well, I think it hardly matters whether it was a conscious move on the part of the early Church Fathers or an instinct, but I expect the Church Fathers were certain that Christianity had to be absolute. Otherwise, it was not going to work. To hold together, there must be no questions—naught but answers. So the Gnostics were directly offensive to the Church Fathers. It seems as if they certainly agree with what some of us are saying today: that there are no answers. There are only questions. The mark of a good society, a few of us might argue, speaking of a society that has not yet come into existence, is that you move from one set of questions up to a higher level of questions. Whereas the early Christian philosophers founded their church upon the opposed conclusion. People must be given absolute certainty about life and death—particularly about death. An absolute statement of Heaven and Hell was required. The notion of reincarnation was too nuanced, too special, too elegant, too delicate, too possible. So it had to be absolutely forbidden and today, for Fundamentalists, is still off the board.

I was reading Nietzsche's *Anti-Christ* a few days ago, and at a certain point he says, "All priests are liars." It's a marvelous remark because it happens to be not only daring but true. Whenever you speak with absolute authority about something that you cannot prove, the decision to speak with such authority means that you are ready to live as a liar. It seems to me that Christianity, because of its determination to be wholly authoritative, was able ultimately to create huge societies. Now, these huge societies work by half, and by half they fail. Certainly, for centuries, they functioned well enough to limp along philosophically full of unanswerable questions, hideous inequalities, and clouds of mendacity, ready to sweep all unanswerable questions under a rug of absolute faith.

Long before the Gnostics, it was taken for granted that there were many gods. This is certainly true of the Egyptians and of the

Greeks. The Hindus believed in a variety of deities. The Africans reacted to all kinds of spirits, high and low. It is as if Judaism and then Christianity came to a contrary conclusion; this plethora of gods did not serve their faiths. It would be better for humans to believe there was one truth only.

And one God, which would of course explain the intensity of the early Christian attacks on the Gnostics.

Yes, they burned their books, they expelled them, they killed them. You know, when they found the Gnostic Gospels in 1945 in Egypt, those were remarkable documents—third- or fourth-century copies of documents that went back to the time of Christ. Elsewhere they had been systematically burned and destroyed. But because of the obscurity of this hiding place, these scrolls had not been uncovered, and so it was a great revelation. Historical and biblical scholars had always known about the Gnostics but mainly because Augustine and Irenaeus had attacked them. They never heard them speak for themselves. When they found the Gnostic Gospels, they discovered a much different Christianity, one that did not embrace a monolithic God and had a host of negative feelings about the Old Testament and the intensity of rage and jealousy in Jehovah. We can ask: What was he jealous of? Maybe other gods. So the Gnostics became the losers in this huge struggle.

But you could see—at least personally I see in the narrowness and the Orthodoxy of Christianity from the time of Augustine on— how narrow Christianity is in relation to its roots: a hatred of the flesh, the concept of Original Sin, the insistence that Jesus must be God. He cannot merely be God's messenger. Such remarkable figures did come out of the Middle East—John the Baptist, Jesus,

Mani, Zoroaster, Adonis, Dionysus, Osiris—incredible figures. From a Gnostic point of view, they would all be messengers sent down to keep alive the spark.

Wouldn't it also be an early attempt to understand the mechanics of existence? I would even say that this curiosity about the nature of God was seen by Judaism and Christianity as the great enemy. You cannot build a powerfully structured society so long as there are all too many ways to elaborate the details. The Judeo-Christian enterprise was determined then to become an absolute arbiter over the more mysterious elements of existence.

And should there be a debate, it was to be resolved by the supreme leaders of the Church.

Yes, do not look into yourself. Refer to your external authority.

And so you could say that the final expression of this was in 1870, when the Catholic Church came up with the infallibility of the Pope. That was always implicit. But finally they now had to state it. It was the final consolidation of Papal power. When you think of the world that was in existence around the time of the birth of Christ, you had two prevailing religious visions—in the Middle East, at any rate: the Greek and the Judaic. They were opposed to each other in a variety of ways and complemented each other in other ways. Christianity can be seen as the synthesis of many of those ideas.

Wasn't Judaism more of a complete religion? On the other hand, Judaism was relatively small. To explain how a Christian sect of Judaism took over that much of the Western world in a few centuries it is necessary, I think, to assume that Rome was at the core of that development. If Rome hadn't existed, one could suspect that Gnosticism might have continued. Gnosticism, after all, had to be congenial to many upper-class Romans. That would be my guess.

Yes.

It gave them a chance to explore themselves. When people are wealthy, they want to do just that. But there were other leaders in Rome who believed that Rome had to become the final answer to existence—Rome and its government. Some even saw that with the aid of Christianity they could fortify authoritative government. Existence could be dictated from the top down. They could even overcome their own upper classes. So this becomes my assumption: It took the Romans to recognize that belief in Jesus Christ was going to be very good for Rome. Immediately, however, this was far from happening. In the first centuries after Christ, Christianity softened Romans. Compassion, after all, was at the core of these new beliefs. Nonetheless, the fundamental Roman concept—that it was vital to have an immensely powerful government at the top—did prevail. And Rome became the seedbed of the idea in the Middle Ages that for society to exist, there must be absolute authority wielded at the center of the summit.

Perhaps without this Roman spur to centrality, our civilization could not have been built. In that sense, the authoritative lie, the New Testament, upon which Christianity was founded did create Western civilization—even if it took twelve centuries to reach the Renaissance. I expect it took so

long because the lie implicit in this new theologically or-
dained faith, this respect for order from above, did present
built-in obstacles. The finest minds were obliged to believe in
dogma. Their lives, after all, were at stake—which can account for the philosophical distances they traveled to make
the illogic of faith palatable to themselves. Medieval philosophy became a study of the ways in which you can arrive at
your desired end by the most special means of language,
which enable you to come out at the end with an affirmation
of mighty oxymorons—as, for example, God is All-Good and
All-Powerful, which, of course, violates not only our own experience but our sense of history. All we can know or feel are
intimations that something did create us.

There is also our philosophical sense that it is far more difficult to explain our existence by the absence of a first cause
than as the consequence of one. Yes, it is not because of anything I read, nor anything I have been taught, certainly not
because of what spiritual propagandists have been trying to
put in my head all these years. No, I believe there is a Creator
because that makes more sense to me. If there is not a God,
then I cannot conceive of how our universe came to be. So I
go on from there to say that if there is such a God, I have to
assume that He or She is not perfect. Not on the aforesaid
basis of one's own experience and the world's experience.
With that, we blunder forward into further intimations of existence, not knowing whether there are forces in existence
larger than our God. Quite possibly, there are. And so the
reason we are having these dialogues—and I cringe at the ongoing crudity necessarily inherent in such brusque presenta-

tion of such sensitive ideas; nonetheless, it is what I can now offer—the reason we are having these dialogues is that Fundamentalist notions of absolute authority are too much of a manic faith machine capable of inspiring world disasters. There was a period, let's say, when without Fundamentalism there might not have been a civilization. That period is now gone. In our age, those same ideas are choking us, distorting us, perverting and blinding us. Just turn on your TV and listen to televangelists yelling for faith and money. Their presence is so toxic that I feel ready to dismiss the eloquent and exceptional rationale of the best theologians and philosophers of the past. I have to add that their need to justify the very improbable propositions that make the televangelists possible also makes the more serious theologies go through excruciating intellectual gymnastics. Embarking on an immense error demands special powers of development in the brain of the person who is working on that vast error. Even though they fail ultimately (and so egregiously that we have had to pay for their failures through the centuries), nonetheless, the powers of human ratiocination have been increased. That is part of the perversity of philosophy. Working with an ill-founded thesis can also improve one's ability to cogitate and debate.

So I guess from what you've said you now understand why here and there in commentary on your work people will say, "Oh, Mailer, he's sort of a Gnostic."

Well, yes, perhaps I do understand— I will say that I want to accomplish something with these dialogues. Normally, you

are not supposed to talk about religion until you know a good
deal about it, and then you are still wise to say little. But I
have proceeded to ponder these questions without being
qualified. Yet my basic argument is that of course I am qualified all the same. We all are. That is why I can say yes, if you
want to get down to it, I probably am a Gnostic in the sense
that the inner feeling I have about these matters is so clear
and so acute to me. I certainly do feel ready to talk about it.
Indeed, I would go so far as to say that oxymorons pollute
the mind, and the Great Oxymoron—All-Good and All-
Powerful—is the most virulent of all, which is equal to saying
that modern-day Fundamentalism is poison to the human
spirit.

Whereas Gnosticism now indicates the road to take?

Perhaps we can now afford to be Gnostics. In early Christian time, the fundamental wisdom of human beings may
have been: "We need order. We do not need stimulation. We
do not need thought that is lively and novel and new. We
need order. We need command from above." That was a
stage in human existence. It was much like the stages of existence that children pass through, where they must live under
order at a certain point or nothing holds their behavior together.

You're talking like a Hegelian now.

Well, I don't care about the labels. I think we are at a stage
of development where Gnosticism may serve us better.

I can imagine how you as a new Gnostic must think about corporations, too.

Well, we don't have to go there. Right now, I much prefer to wander through the forests of theology than the quicksands of economics. Let me conclude, however, by thanking you for the order and stimulation you brought to this theologically ignorant mind.

X

Prayer

MICHAEL LENNON: *Here's a question on ritual. It will introduce us to the question of prayer. All your ideas, I would say, have an underlying assumption that God has a continuing, even a profound interest in some individuals and certainly in the ultimate fate of the human species, flora and fauna, and the rest of His Creation. This is completely at odds with some of the earliest recorded religious expression, namely, from the Sumerians, whose prayers were always begging the gods, "Remember!" Prayer and ritual were a constant attempt to engage the attention of forgetful and indifferent gods who had created but had abandoned humanity. This, by the way, wasn't a notion emerging from disasters and dislocations but could be found even as their civilization flourished. Can you comment?*

NORMAN MAILER: It's the other half of the equation. The obverse side of prayer is that it rarely gets answered—so rarely, indeed, that people at religious meetings cite such events as formidable. Answered prayers are often seen as a species of miracle. Prayers are not usually answered. But then I think of the Lord wading through a mud wash of prayers: "Oh, God, let my team win the game!" "Oh, God, let me sell this old heap that no one wants so I can buy a new heap with spoke wheels."

I don't think God listens to prayer. The Sumerians, as you describe them, were relatively sophisticated people who recognized that they might pray, but answers did not come often.

Now let's suppose some people have a child who's ill, and they pray to God with great sincerity, begging for their child to live. I'm willing to accept the effort as not something to sneer at. I won't say it works, but we can certainly feel for the parent.

When you were talking about Gandhi and oxymorons, you said: "There are a few that are vital and valuable. One of them is 'heroic passivity.' There, one's experience must serve as the arbiter. There can be heroic passivity, or quasi-passivity. The latter can be a disaster." Along that line, what would you say about the contemplative life? By that I mean the cloistered orders who don't run hospitals or schools, just pray for the world. This is a strong Christian tradition, ditto for the Buddhists and some Hindus, and probably Hasidim engage in some variant of that. Do you see a value in this kind of passivity?

I would answer yes. I'm not opposed. If we're going to come nearer to God, to find a sense of God behind the words, it's perfectly conceivable to me that the deity of whom I speak does pay attention to transcendental sincerity. I have a crude analogy to offer. Occasionally, after having worked on a novel, you come across a review that's so intelligently written and gets so close to what you were attempting to do or, even better, offers insights you did not arrive at by yourself that your work is more illuminated for you. Such a critic makes me feel better about the act of writing. So do I also think that there are people who contemplate existence, then pray in depth to God and are qualified to do so. They are not petty. What I hate about prayer is that so often it is superficial and greedy. Most of the time it is looking for an undeserved advantage: I'm kind of stupid, God, but maybe You'll help me because I'm praying to You. They do it as if modesty is the only passport needed.

This is about Buddhism: What's your take on the Buddhist notion of the boddhisatva vow? Reaching nirvana is a catch-22: If you have achieved a level of deep compassion, enough to reach nirvana, you can't go happily off into it while other sentient beings are still here struggling and suffering. So even though you personally have a free pass out of this far-from-perfect world, you voluntarily reincarnate as a boddhisatva—a helper, a teacher, a guide to the way—and keep reincarnating until everyone has achieved nirvana. Devout Buddhist lay people of many persuasions, and all the monks and nuns, take the "bodhisattva vow" at an advanced stage of their training.

It's a beautiful notion. The difficulty I've always had with Buddhism, however, is not bodhisattva but nirvana. As I see it, the point of existence is not to rise above our petty feelings and leave them behind but, on the contrary, to be able to struggle with those petty feelings in such a way that we lift them into more vigorous feelings. Nirvana always struck me as a place I had no interest in reaching. Whether it existed or not—I had no idea—it did not appeal. I remember talking to a friend of mine who's a good Buddhist, and I soon fell into a polite rage. Over just a few drinks! "You Buddhists always talk about nothingness, at how to arrive at nothingness," I told him, and added, "As a writer, I can tell you, I live with nothingness every minute I'm working. I sit at my desk and for the first half hour there's nothing—I have to pass through such nothingness in order to come to a few ideas. You're not really talking about nothingness. Nothingness is an awful state! It's so empty a state. Why don't you talk about what it really is you are looking for, which is *the ineffable*?"

I hope he was struck with the thought, even if only by a little. Being a good Buddhist, he did no more than smile!

Back to the bodhisattva: I would say again it's a noble conception. Whether true or not is another matter.

At the end of one of our interviews, you said that in many ways the Creator might be comparable to a Greek god—strong yet not All-Powerful, flawed but noble; well, you know, Greek myths are full of incidents where the gods took human form or animal form. Apart from the well-known stories of Zeus turning up as this or that personage to impregnate some female, there are also stories of Zeus

turning up as a beggar. In one story, peasants take in a wretched
beggar overnight, share their far-from-abundant meal with him,
treat him very well, and next morning find his bed empty and a
sack of gold in his place—Zeus came calling and rewarded them for
their kindness to the poor! God showing up on earth is an idea em-
braced long before Christian theology.

I don't see any need to answer the question. I just take it
for granted. If God wants to appear as a human, indeed He
would. But I think what's more interesting is the belief that if
you're good when you don't have to be good, something favorable can happen, which I think is also part of human nature. Humans live for revenge—but they also live for the
belief that we are capable of goodness. For me, the brunt of
these stories is the human desire involved. I want to be capable of goodness, and indeed I would also wish to believe that
there is something in the universe that will reward you for
goodness. Prayer, I would argue, is all too often the stepchild
of that emotion.

I want to go back to a crucial point. Earlier you said you doubted the
efficacy of prayers because all too often they were requests for per-
sonal gains or status: money, a job, a new car. But do you give
enough credence to the huge number of people who pray for guid-
ance or forgiveness or for strength to avoid sin? These types of
prayers may exceed the greedy type. Who could say?

I would agree. Let us even assume they do exceed it. My
point is that God may not pay great attention to most prayer.
Think of it as an immensely abused communication system,
which is overwhelmingly present in human affairs. I would

suppose that God can pick up human messages without the need for prayer. I will admit that a prayer can have, on occasion, such vibrancy that God is cheered by it. But I would also say that most prayer is wasteful and self-indulgent, an exercise in narcissism. Over the years, I've heard so many people say, "I'm praying for you." My reaction is, "I don't need it. It's not helping. You're just invading my presence." Often, it is no more than another petty human weapon. It could be well intended. They do care about you, they want to do the best they can for you. But do they really need to pray to make their feelings legitimate? If they love you, then you are probably going to reap a benefit whether they try to talk to God or not.

How so?

Through the warmth you receive from them—the honest warmth of their feeling rather than the oratorical "I'll pray for you."

You feel then that prayer tends to be meretricious?

That may be too strong a word. How about oversubscribed? Ninety percent of prayer may not necessarily lead to anything. I think a lot of people pray in order to intensify their sense of focus. They are doing it for themselves. What I don't like about prayer is the enormous baggage that goes with it, the stultification of society that is shored up by prayer, the number of mediocrities who pray for something that they know nothing about. You can see humongous examples of that on television every night, crowd-rousers invoking the holy efficacy of prayer while seizing every false advantage they can find—including, how not?—quick appeals for money.

Static.

Worse. I think the interception of prayer may be one of the Devil's most powerful instruments. Whenever a prayer is offered that is lacking whole integrity, the Devil may know how to profit from such shoddy work.

Many religious people find solace in praying together. They believe that group prayer, at a religious service or in a group of people, is a more efficacious way of reaching the Lord. Now, the Lord may be too engaged to pick up a single cry for intercession, but he can hardly neglect a full house of prayers from, say, St. Peter's, led by the Pope on the son's birthday. Quantity changes quality, as you are forever saying.

There is no question in my mind that St. Peter's would attract God's attention. Still, we must enter into the nature of the communal prayer. For example, right now, a war is being waged between Islam and ourselves. If there is a particular phenomenon that characterizes Islam, it is how they pray together five times a day. They put their foreheads to the ground, they raise their buttocks toward Heaven, and they pray. And we in the West look down on it. We tend to consider that kind of excessive. Moreover, we don't necessarily believe that Allah is well-intentioned. To us, he is an alien God. So the fact that a number of people get together for such prayer and have a community of opinion doesn't make them appear virtuous to us. For that matter—change of venue!—when a theater audience laughs as one, does that have any relation to prayer? To feel that one is part of a great group of people is reassuring regardless of the occasion. But whether prayer is beneficial is quite another matter. All over America there are now prayers to Christ for our soldiers in Iraq, whole communities praying that our soldiers don't run their Humvees over terrorists' explosives. Of course, you've also got Islamics praying just as powerfully and just as intently that their enemies will be wiped out by the same explosives.

Why not also say that the people at St. Peter's may be praying for us to get out of that war?

All right. Exactly. Some are. And I can believe there is a collective telepathic power that humans do have. With a thousand people together, or ten thousand, yes, the effect may be magnified beyond the numbers. But to assume it is magnified to good purpose is a very large assumption. It could as easily be toward an evil one. Humans are skewed away from the point all the time. America spent close to fifty years believing that Russia was the evil empire while all the time that ugly, cruel place was getting weaker and weaker and growing worse and worse as it became less capable of destroying us. For the last two decades of the Soviets, we never saw them for what they were: a constipated commerce-locked economy, an overordered society, slow in development, and, in relation to us, as boastful as it was empty. Their real desire may have been to rise to some beginning of economic equality with us. They lacked the inner wherewithal to believe they could destroy us, and all the while our anti-Sovietism served the needs of the American power seekers. We kept the American public afraid of the Soviets long after it may have been justifiable. By the end, they were not the evil empire but a wretched kingdom.

We were praying against it, too, praying for its collapse.

We weren't praying for its collapse. We were hoping that when a war came we would destroy the Russians before they would destroy us.

But when we read in the newspapers about what was going on in Russia in the seventies and eighties and how grim it was, I'm sure a lot of people were saying, "The Lord is bringing the Russians to their knees."

Well, now you have a great many people saying, "Maybe the Lord will bring Islam to its knees." Islam is saying, "Allah will bring the great Satan to its knees." The notion that a country is holy or evil, I find insupportable.

Right. Even in the Islamic world we know there is such a chasm between the Sunnis and the Shiites. Their detestation of each other is profound.

They certainly outdo the old animosity between the Catholics and the Protestants.

You've spoken about dreams being a contested field. That is, divine and demonic forces use dreams to send their messages to humans. If

this is true, why can't God and the Devil also communicate Their
messages to a mind seeking a line of communication with something
transcendental? I assume you believe that humans can pray to the
Devil as easily as to the Lord.

Unwittingly. Let me put it this way: I think people who
believe in the Devil have ceremonies that are not exactly
prayer but more like invocations. There may be a fundamental concept in magical groups that you don't reach the Devil
by praying to Him or Her. You invoke such a presence. I
would say that the tendency in Christianity, all exceptions
noted, is to pray to God rather than invoke Him.

Does your belief in karma have anything to do with your less-than-
enthusiastic feelings about prayer?

I think I would say that if you live a life that is a little better,
a little braver, a little more compassionate or responsible than
what was expected of you, you may well be taken care of in
your rebirth. This assumes that a foul-up in communication
does not occur in reincarnation, but of that one can hardly be
certain. In any event, let me argue that attention to one's karma
is a grand substitute for prayer, a real and legitimate and profound substitute for prayer. Nonetheless, I can see exceptional
cases where a prayer is so beautiful and comes out of such
depth in a human and has such inner resonance that divine attention is paid. But I think such prayers are as rare as the work
of a fine artist. Let me add that you don't have to be an edu-
cated person to have a beautiful prayer. Such a prayer comes
out of the depths of your experience and shows a hard-earned
balance of perception and passion, of forgiveness and true

human need. Such elements can form an exceptional unity. We can understand a parent praying for the health of a sick child and find it honorable and true whether the prayer is heard or not, honorable because of the intensity and focus of the love.

You are arguing then that if prayer is to be efficacious or to be heard at all, it has to be all of those things you said: whole, pure, and free of cynicisms.

And best of all, free of motive that is concealed from one's self.

The saints can also be addressed in prayer.

For Catholics.

For some Protestants, too, Episcopalians.

It seems to me that Catholics have about five times as many saints as the Protestants. Is that true?

Well, they do have a lot of saints. But there are some that Episcopals will recognize. Obviously, if there is a Heaven and there are as many people up there as Christians think there are, untold numbers of saints are to be found in Heaven. However, to know for certain that someone is in Heaven, that's the definition of a saint.

Among Catholics? Literally?

Literally. Among Fundamentalists you almost never hear about individual saints.

Jesus is the all-purpose saint for Baptists. God, archangel, saint, lawgiver, cheerleader, and coach all in one. I suspect that the mental and spiritual benefits that some good, honest people receive from referring in their thoughts to a particular saint come because that helps to bring some kind of focus to their problem. That is one more reason why the Church lasted two thousand years but, not being a Catholic, I feel equally that the distortions of existence that accompany Catholicism are immense. I am not, however, going to say that the Church has not been good for a good many people in a good many ways, yet it has also stomped upon human imagination. So I would go so far as to say that Catholicism ultimately may be stultifying to God and is half possessed by the Devil. I would say as much for any other established religion. I don't need Catholicism to be the villain. All organized churches and synagogues are, in that sense, obfuscations to separate us from a closer sense of the nature of God.

But you have talked about God's involvement in some of the great religions over the years.

How not? But what about the Devil's involvement? And the congregation? There they are, fighting it out in the alleys and on the altars of religion. There is not a seminary in the world of whatever persuasion where you don't have God and the Devil working day and night right down into the acolyte's genitals—the temptations, the agonies, the repressions, the wonders. How many fine seminarians have to wonder, finally, whether they are working for God or the Devil? Can one even be a fine seminarian without some concern over that?

To conclude—can you begin to explain why so many people do pray?

The act is obviously cleansing for a good many. It requires some concentration on what is one's greatest need at the moment and what might be one's greatest hope. It can encourage modesty in men and women who are vain and perhaps even inspire courage in a few. Prayer can also enable one to come closer to what is most awful in oneself. Prayer can offer the only solace available when grief is overwhelming. All of those positive elements can be present. What I distrust, however, is the notion that prayers will certainly be heard on high and thereby will prove efficacious. Believe in that as a fact, and one is back in the depth of century-old superstitions that left our minds circling endlessly around the same empty intellectual places. It's a mystery, so don't think about it. Be philosophical! That was the theological comfort you were offered.

AFTERWORD

NORMAN MAILER: To shift the course of this discussion, there are some remarks I have been thinking about for some time with which I would like to conclude. Part of the interest I've had in theology has been political. If I pose the question "What kind of political system would God like?" I'm not convinced God is certain. In different times, the heavens may have been partial to monarchy, to communism, and certainly the Lord was interested in democracy, in capitalism. (As was the Devil!) These systems are not without comparison to the designs of God's animals. Which ones turn out best? I think a great deal was put into communism at one point. However, I also have this notion that the Devil is at war with God, so, even as communism ended badly, democracy could end badly. It's why I speak of an existential God.

You may ask: Where is the positive element in all this? How can politics give us a sense of beauty, awe, or even a feeling that we might want to be nearer to God? What do people like me believe in this vein? What are my positive intimations of God as a political presence? Well, I do believe there are elements of compassion in our political world, elements of goodness. It is not difficult to believe that love is more of a life-giving force than hate. The majority of us are working, after all, to create a world where there is reasonable equity. What political form could that world take? If we start with the brilliant forays of writers as great as Nietzsche, we would have to argue that it is wrong to pay great attention to the weak, the poor, the hungry, the meek, the mediocre, the inferior. They are, Nietzsche declares, a prodigious deadweight upon existence. Filled with hatred, they wish to destroy all that is noble or aristocratic, beautiful or fine. It is a sustainable argument— Nietzsche is probably the most talented and powerful conservative of them all. Yet as a thesis, it goes only just so far before it crashes, and that is for a very simple reason: The aristocracy was corrupt, as were the theologians and the oligarchs of capitalism. Conservatism is as filthy in its practices as its leftist opponents. If the poor are malodorous, so are the rich. And the rich have advantages that the poor do not have.

On the other hand, even at its best, socialism has never worked too well. Why? Because it refuses to live with the notion that God exists and is part of the human balance. So a built-in paradox intrudes on what was conceived as an open, equitable system. It is that the majority of leaders who come to power under socialism do not believe in the existence of

God and are soon engaged in personal competitions, rivalry, and finally the overriding impulse to be the sole leader—yes, who will have the prevailing ego? My feeling, then, is that to advocate socialism without some sense that religion may also have to be the foundation itself may be to make a profound error.

The beauty of Christ—what Christ was saying to all of us—is that the poor have as much reason to exist as the wealthy. I don't want to oversimplify Nietzsche's argument, but finally he did feel that Christ was not only speaking to the unwashed but arousing a great rage in them, and this rage would yet destroy all that was first-rate in civilization. I would argue that unless we have some real understanding of the needs of the poor, and the rights of the poor, plus the passion of the poor to become more than they have been condemned to be for generations, we are only looking to bypass the horrors of society. I would also say that socialism without belief in an existential God cannot offer real riches to human illumination. Whereas socialism accompanied by belief in a God who wants much of what we want can liberate society for us. So I suppose that if a socialist society should ever come into being with a belief in an existential God, I think we might begin to find some more developed stirrings of human equity.

Let me say, since I have a great distrust of large organizations and monumental government power, that I also think small business must be a viable part of any existential socialism. Let the largest organizations be socialist rather than corporate, because the corporations cannot be trusted. The corporation is—I've called it the Big Empty. The corporation

is psychopathic. It does not care about its past; it has very little interest in its previous history; it has very little interest in
its future.

MICHAEL LENNON: *It does have an interest in its future.*

Things are done without looking to the long future. For
example, outsourcing is an immediate way of making profits.
So many are obliged to show a profit every year, just like the
psychopath has to feel that he and his ego are larger today
than yesterday. Otherwise, they will go into a depression. By
contrast, under existential socialism, it would be natural to
have an interest in the past and the future. The idea: You
don't look for huge profits but for the gradually increasing
well-being of all, the ongoing enrichment of culture. To keep
such socialism alive, small business has to be encouraged, and
the notion of community, of neighborhood. For small business may be more innovative than socialism, more on a par
with inventors, artist, gamblers, and adventurers and teach-
ers, more in proportion to the scope of human wit—whereas
the concerns of corporate management are for power and
profit, exceptional overweening profit for the top.

Behind an existential socialism with some open regard for
small business stirs the idea that we might even be working
with God. Not working to obey Him, to praise Him, to slave
for His vanity, but on the contrary, to live with the idea that
God does share desires with us, that we are at last working together, yes, finally—after millennia of hatred of God, be-
seechments of God, intense if mindless prayer, sloughs and

promontories of ritual, attempts to work for God and oneself by inquisitorial force, attempts to do without God, attempts to glorify Him at the expense of all reason—there might be at last an agreeable sense that, yes, we might be working with the deity, and He might be working with us. If we don't understand God in large part, God, in turn, may not understand us altogether. Yet we might even develop the beginnings of a real and nourishing regard for each other. So one would postulate a society built on the lively concept that God needs us as much as we need God. I would say that premise offers more promise than the ongoing overinflated managerial ethic of corporate capitalism so ready to believe that greed is good and full of God's sanction, and that the free market is Valhalla. Yet how much more life could be gained by the opposed belief that in company (at least some of the time) with the Creator, we can try to do the best of which we are capable, even as we navigate the falls, the rapids, the rocks, and the unforeseen events of our ongoing experience.

APPRECIATIONS

The authors would like to thank Eugene Kennedy and Robert Klaus for their criticisms and contributions to this book. They are not, of course, to be identified with any of its arguments.

NORMAN MAILER was born in Brooklyn in 1923. His first book, *The Naked and the Dead*, was published in 1948, instantly making him one of the most celebrated writers to emerge after World War II. In a career spanning almost sixty years, he wrote thirty-seven books of fiction, nonfiction, essays, poetry, and criticism. In 1969 he won the National Book Award and the Pulitzer Prize for *The Armies of the Night*. Mailer received another Pulitzer in 1980 for *The Executioner's Song*. For many years he lived in Provincetown, Massachusetts, with his wife, Norris Church Mailer. He died on November 10, 2007, in New York City.

MICHAEL LENNON is emeritus professor of English at Wilkes University in Pennsylvania and serves as Norman Mailer's archivist, authorized biographer, and one of his literary executors. The author or editor of six books on Mailer's works, he is the president of the Norman Mailer Society. He lives in Westport, Massachusetts.